Get Ready!

FOR STANDARDIZED TESTS

READING, GRADE FOUR

TEST PREPARATION SERIES

Get Ready!

FOR STANDARDIZED TESTS

READING, GRADE FOUR

Kris Callahan

Carol Turkington
Series Editor

McGraw-Hill

New York   Chicago   San Francisco
Lisbon   London   Madrid   Mexico City
Milan   New Delhi   San Juan   Seoul
Singapore   Sydney   Toronto

Library of Congress Cataloging-in-Publication Data

Get ready! for standardized tests. Reading.
    p. cm.—(Test preparation series)
  Contents:—[v. 2] Grade two / Louise Ulrich—[v. 3] Grade three / Joanne Baker—
[v. 4] Grade four / Kris Callahan.
   ISBN 0-07-137406-X (pbk. : v. 2)—ISBN 0-07-137407-8 (pbk. : v. 3)—ISBN
0-07-137408-6 (pbk. : v. 4)
   1. Achievement tests—United States—Study guides. 2. Reading (Elementary)—United
States—Evaluation. 3. Reading (Elementary)—Parent participation—United States. I.
Ulrich, Louise. II. Test preparation series (McGraw-Hill Companies)

  LB3060.22 .G48 2001
  372.126'2—dc21   2001030896

McGraw-Hill

A Division of The McGraw·Hill Companies

1 2 3 4 5 6 7 8 9 0 COU/COU 0 9 8 7 6 5 4 3 2 1

ISBN 0-07-137408-6

This book was set in New Century Schoolbook by Inkwell Publishing Services.

Printed and bound by Courier.

McGraw-Hill books are available at special quantity discounts to use as premiums
and sales promotions, or for use in corporate training programs. For more information, please write to the Director of Special Sales, McGraw-Hill, Professional
Publishing, Two Penn Plaza, New York, NY 10121-2298. Or contact your local bookstore.

A special thank you to family and friends who believed
in me and encouraged me through this project.
To my kids, past, present, and future:
Remember that Captain Callahan knows you can do it!

Kris Callahan

Contents

SKILLS CHECKLIST

MY CHILD ...	HAS LEARNED	IS WORKING ON
VOCABULARY		
WORD MEANINGS IN CONTEXT		
SYNONYMS		
ANTONYMS		
HOMOPHONES		
ROOT WORDS		
SINGULAR AND PLURAL		
PREFIXES		
SUFFIXES		
COMPOUND WORDS		
CONTRACTIONS		
PARTS OF SPEECH		
PUNCTUATION		
MAIN IDEA		
SEQUENCE		
CHARACTERS		
SETTINGS		
CAUSE AND EFFECT		
COMPARE AND CONTRAST		
PREDICTING OUTCOMES		
DRAWING CONCLUSIONS		
FACTS AND OPINION		
CHARACTER ANALYSIS		
REALITY VERSUS FANTASY		
BIOGRAPHY		
POETRY		
ALPHABETICAL ORDER TO THE THIRD LETTER		
DICTIONARY SKILLS		
GRAPHS		
REFERENCE BOOKS		
RECOGNIZING PARTS OF A BOOK		

Introduction

Almost all of us have taken standardized tests in school. We spent several days bubbling-in answers, shifting in our seats. No one ever told us why we took the tests or what they would do with the results. We just took them and never heard about them again.

Today many parents aren't aware they are entitled to see their children's permanent records and, at a reasonable cost, to obtain copies of any information not protected by copyright, including testing scores. Late in the school year, most parents receive standardized test results with confusing bar charts and detailed explanations of scores that few people seem to understand.

In response to a series of negative reports on the state of education in this country, Americans have begun to demand that something be done to improve our schools. We have come to expect higher levels of accountability as schools face the competing pressures of rising educational expectations and declining school budgets. High-stakes standardized tests are rapidly becoming the main tool of accountability for students, teachers, and school administrators. If students' test scores don't continually rise, teachers and principals face the potential loss of school funding and, ultimately, their jobs. Summer school and private after-school tutorial program enrollments are swelling with students who have not met score standards or who, everyone agrees, could score higher.

While there is a great deal of controversy about whether it is appropriate for schools to use standardized tests to make major decisions about individual students, it appears likely that standardized tests are here to stay. They will be used to evaluate students, teachers, and the schools; schools are sure to continue to use students' test scores to demonstrate their accountability to the community.

The purposes of this guide are to acquaint you with the types of standardized tests your children may take; to help you understand the test results; and to help you work with your children in skill areas that are measured by standardized tests so they can perform as well as possible.

Types of Standardized Tests

The two major types of group standardized tests are *criterion-referenced tests* and *norm-referenced tests*. Think back to when you learned to tie your shoes. First Mom or Dad showed you how to loosen the laces on your shoe so that you could insert your foot; then they showed you how to tighten the laces—but not too tight. They showed you how to make bows and how to tie a knot. All the steps we just described constitute what is called a *skills hierarchy:* a list of skills from easiest to most difficult that are related to some goal, such as tying a shoelace.

Criterion-referenced tests are designed to determine at what level students are performing on various skills hierarchies. These tests assume that development of skills follows a sequence of steps. For example, if you were teaching shoelace tying, the skills hierarchy might appear this way:

1. Loosen laces.
2. Insert foot.
3. Tighten laces.
4. Make loops with both lace ends.
5. Tie a square knot.

Criterion-referenced tests try to identify how far along the skills hierarchy the student has progressed. There is no comparison against any-one else's score, only against an expected skill level. The main question criterion-referenced tests ask is: "Where is this child in the development of this group of skills?"

Norm-referenced tests, in contrast, are typically constructed to compare children in their abilities as to different skills areas. Although the experts who design test items may be aware of skills hierarchies, they are more concerned with how much of some skill the child has mastered, rather than at what level on the skills hierarchy the child is.

Ideally, the questions on these tests range from very easy items to those that are impossibly difficult. The essential feature of norm-referenced tests is that scores on these measures can be compared to scores of children in similar groups. They answer this question: "How does the child compare with other children of the same age or grade placement in the development of this skill?"

This book provides strategies for increasing your child's scores on both standardized norm-referenced and criterion-referenced tests.

The Major Standardized Tests

Many criterion-referenced tests currently in use are created locally or (at best) on a state level,

and there are far too many of them to go into detail here about specific tests. However, children prepare for them in basically the same way they do for norm-referenced tests.

A very small pool of norm-referenced tests is used throughout the country, consisting primarily of the Big Five:

- California Achievement Tests (CTB/McGraw-Hill)
- Iowa Tests of Basic Skills (Riverside)
- Metropolitan Achievement Test (Harcourt-Brace & Company)
- Stanford Achievement Test (Psychological Corporation)
- TerraNova [formerly Comprehensive Test of Basic Skills] (McGraw-Hill)

These tests use various terms for the academic skills areas they assess, but they generally test several types of reading, language, and mathematics skills, along with social studies and science. They may include additional assessments, such as of study and reference skills.

How States Use Standardized Tests

Despite widespread belief and practice to the contrary, group standardized tests are designed to assess and compare the achievement of groups. They are *not* designed to provide detailed diagnostic assessments of individual students. (For detailed individual assessments, children should be given individual diagnostic tests by properly qualified professionals, including trained guidance counselors, speech and language therapists, and school psychologists.) Here are examples of the types of questions group standardized tests are designed to answer:

- How did the reading achievement of students at Valley Elementary School this year compare with their reading achievement last year?

- How did math scores at Wonderland Middle School compare with those of students at Parkside Middle School this year?

- As a group, how did Hilltop High School students compare with the national averages in the achievement areas tested?

- How did the district's first graders' math scores compare with the district's fifth graders' math scores?

The fact that these tests are designed primarily to test and compare groups doesn't mean that test data on individual students isn't useful. It does mean that when we use these tests to diagnose individual students, we are using them for a purpose for which they were not designed.

Think of group standardized tests as being similar to health fairs at the local mall. Rather than check into your local hospital and spend thousands of dollars on full, individual tests for a wide range of conditions, you can go from station to station and take part in different health screenings. Of course, one would never diagnose heart disease or cancer on the basis of the screening done at the mall. At most, suspicious results on the screening would suggest that you need to visit a doctor for a more complete examination.

In the same way, group standardized tests provide a way of screening the achievement of many students quickly. Although you shouldn't diagnose learning problems solely based on the results of these tests, the results can tell you that you should think about referring a child for a more definitive, individual assessment.

An individual student's group test data should be considered only a point of information. Teachers and school administrators may use standardized test results to support or question hypotheses they have made about students; but these scores must be used alongside other information, such as teacher comments, daily work, homework, class test grades, parent observations, medical needs, and social history.

Valid Uses of Standardized Test Scores

Here are examples of appropriate uses of test scores for individual students:

- Mr. Cone thinks that Samantha, a third grader, is struggling in math. He reviews her file and finds that her first- and second-grade standardized test math scores were very low. Her first- and second-grade teachers recall episodes in which Samantha cried because she couldn't understand certain math concepts, and mention that she was teased by other children, who called her "Dummy." Mr. Cone decides to refer Samantha to the school assistance team to determine whether she should be referred for individual testing for a learning disability related to math.

- The local college wants to set up a tutoring program for elementary school children who are struggling academically. In deciding which youngsters to nominate for the program, the teachers consider the students' averages in different subjects, the degree to which students seem to be struggling, parents' reports, and standardized test scores.

- For the second year in a row, Gene has performed poorly on the latest round of standardized tests. His teachers all agree that Gene seems to have some serious learning problems. They had hoped that Gene was immature for his class and that he would do better this year; but his dismal grades continue. Gene is referred to the school assistance team to determine whether he should be sent to the school psychologist for assessment of a possible learning handicap.

Inappropriate Use of Standardized Test Scores

Here are examples of how schools have sometimes used standardized test results inappropriately:

- Mr. Johnson groups his students into reading groups solely on the basis of their standardized test scores.

- Ms. Henry recommends that Susie be held back a year because she performed poorly on the standardized tests, despite strong grades on daily assignments, homework, and class tests.

- Gerald's teacher refers him for consideration in the district's gifted program, which accepts students using a combination of intelligence test scores, achievement test scores, and teacher recommendations. Gerald's intelligence test scores were very high. Unfortunately, he had a bad cold during the week of the standardized group achievement tests and was taking powerful antihistamines, which made him feel sleepy. As a result, he scored too low on the achievement tests to qualify.

The public has come to demand increasingly high levels of accountability for public schools. We demand that schools test so that we have hard data with which to hold the schools accountable. But too often, politicians and the public place more faith in the test results than is justified. Regardless of whether it's appropriate to do so and regardless of the reasons schools use standardized test results as they do, many schools base crucial programming and eligibility decisions on scores from group standardized tests. It's to your child's advantage, then, to perform as well as possible on these tests.

Two Basic Assumptions

The strategies we present in this book come from two basic assumptions:

1. Most students can raise their standardized test scores.

2. Parents can help their children become stronger in the skills the tests assess.

This book provides the information you need to learn what skill areas the tests measure, what general skills your child is being taught in a particular grade, how to prepare your child to take the tests, and what to do with the results. In the appendices you will find information to help you decipher test interpretations; a listing of which states currently require what tests; and additional resources to help you help your child to do better in school and to prepare for the tests.

A Word about Coaching

This guide is *not* about coaching your child. When we use the term *coaching* in referring to standardized testing, we mean trying to give someone an unfair advantage, either by revealing beforehand what exact items will be on the test or by teaching "tricks" that will supposedly allow a student to take advantage of some detail in how the tests are constructed.

Some people try to coach students in shrewd test-taking strategies that take advantage of how the tests are supposedly constructed rather than strengthening the students' skills in the areas tested. Over the years, for example, many rumors have been floated about "secret formulas" that test companies use.

This type of coaching emphasizes ways to help students obtain scores they didn't earn—to get something for nothing. Stories have appeared in the press about teachers who have coached their students on specific questions, parents who have tried to obtain advance copies of tests, and students who have written down test questions after taking standardized tests and sold them to others. Because of the importance of test security, test companies and states aggressively prosecute those who attempt to violate test security—and they should do so.

How to Raise Test Scores

Factors that are unrelated to how strong students are but that might artificially lower test scores include anything that prevents students from making scores that accurately describe their actual abilities. Some of those factors are:

- giving the tests in uncomfortably cold or hot rooms;

- allowing outside noises to interfere with test taking; and

- reproducing test booklets in such small print or with such faint ink that students can't read the questions.

Such problems require administrative attention from both the test publishers, who must make sure that they obtain their norms for the tests under the same conditions students face when they take the tests; and school administrators, who must ensure that conditions under which their students take the tests are as close as possible to those specified by the test publishers.

Individual students also face problems that can artificially lower their test scores, and parents can do something about many of these problems. Stomach aches, headaches, sleep deprivation, colds and flu, and emotional upsets due to a recent tragedy are problems that might call for the student to take the tests during make-up sessions. Some students have physical conditions such as muscle-control problems, palsies, or difficulty paying attention that require work over many months or even years before students can obtain accurate test scores on standardized tests. And, of course, some students just don't take the testing seriously or may even intentionally perform poorly. Parents can help their children overcome many of these obstacles to obtaining accurate scores.

Finally, with this book parents are able to help their children raise their scores by:

- increasing their familiarity (and their comfort level) with the types of questions on standardized tests;

- drills and practice exercises to increase their skill in handling the kinds of questions they will meet; and

- providing lots of fun ways for parents to help their children work on the skill areas that will be tested.

Test Questions

The favorite type of question for standardized tests is the multiple-choice question. For example:

1. The first President of the United States was:

    A Abraham Lincoln

    B Martin Luther King, Jr.

    C George Washington

    D Thomas Jefferson

The main advantage of multiple-choice questions is that it is easy to score them quickly and accurately. They lend themselves to optical scanning test forms, on which students fill in bubbles or squares and the forms are scored by machine. Increasingly, companies are moving from paper-based testing to computer-based testing, using multiple-choice questions.

The main disadvantage of multiple-choice questions is that they restrict test items to those that can be put in that form. Many educators and civil rights advocates have noted that the multiple-choice format only reveals a superficial understanding of the subject. It's not possible with multiple-choice questions to test a student's ability to construct a detailed, logical argument on some issue or to explain a detailed process. Although some of the major tests are beginning to incorporate more subjectively scored items, such as short answer or essay questions, the vast majority of test items continue to be in multiple-choice format.

In the past, some people believed there were special formulas or tricks to help test-takers determine which multiple-choice answer was the correct one. There may have been some truth to *some* claims for past tests. Computer analyses of some past tests revealed certain biases in how tests were constructed. For example, the old advice to pick *D* when in doubt appears to have been valid for some past tests. However, test publishers have become so sophisticated in their ability to detect patterns of bias in the formulation of test questions and answers that they now guard against it aggressively.

In Chapter 1, we provide information about general test-taking considerations, with advice on how parents can help students overcome testing obstacles. The rest of the book provides information to help parents help their children strengthen skills in the tested areas.

Joseph Harris, Ph.D.

Test-Taking Basics

It's almost certain that some time during the 12 years that your child spends in school, he will face a standardized testing situation. Some schools test every year, some test every other year or every three years, but nearly all schools use some form of standardized testing for assessment purposes. How well your child does on this type of test can be related to many things. For example, did he get plenty of rest the night before? Is he anxious in testing situations? Did he get confused when filling in the answer sheets and mark the wrong bubble by mistake? Because children so often have problems with the mechanics of testing, educators do not use these tests as sole criterion for judging how well a child is learning and developing. Instead, the scores are only one part of the educational picture, the other part consisting of the child's classroom performance. That said, however, standardized tests can enable parents and teachers to see a general pattern of strengths and weaknesses.

What This Book Can Do

This book is not designed to help your child artificially inflate his scores on a standardized test. Instead, its purpose is to help you understand the typical kinds of skills taught in a fourth-grade class and what a typical fourth grader can be expected to know by the end of the fourth year. It presents lots of fun activities that you can use at home to work with your child in particular skill areas that may be a bit weak.

This book is not designed to replace your child's teacher, but as a guide to help you work together with the school as a team to help your child succeed.

Keep in mind, however, that endless drilling is not the best way to help your child improve. Most children want to do well and please their teachers and parents, but they already spend about seven hours a day in school. Extracurricular activities, homework, music, and sports practice take up more time. To avoid overwhelming your child, try to use the activities in this book to stimulate and support your children's work at school.

Children entering the fourth grade are usually independent thinkers who can handle more complex material in school than they have been able to process in the past. As a result of the changes in the way your child thinks, you'll find he is better able to remember complex material and to begin to summarize effectively. But remember that not all children learn things at the same rate. What may be typical for one fourth grader is certainly not for another. You should use the information presented in this book as only a general developmental guideline while focusing on your child's actual schoolwork to help him develop his essential skills in reading, grammar, and writing.

How to Use This Book

There are many different ways to use this book. Some children are quite strong in certain verbal areas, but they need a bit of help in other areas. Perhaps your child is a whiz at vocabulary but has some trouble with reading comprehension. Focus your time and attention on the weaker skills that need some work.

You'll see in each chapter an introductory explanation of the material in the chapter, followed by a summary of what a typical child in fourth grade should be expected to know in that content area by the end of the year. This is followed in each chapter by an extensive section featuring interesting, fun, or unusual activities you can do with your child to reinforce the skills presented in the chapter. Most use only inexpensive items found around the home, and many are suitable for car trips, waiting rooms, and restaurants. Next, you'll find an explanation of how typical standardized tests may assess these skills and what your child might expect to see on a typical test.

We've included sample questions at the end of each section that are designed to help familiarize your child with the types of questions found on a typical standardized test. These questions do **not** measure your child's proficiency in any given content area, but if you notice your child is having trouble with a particular question, you can use that information to figure out what skills you need to focus on.

Basic Test-Taking Strategies

Sometimes children score lower on standardized tests because they approach testing in an inefficient way. There are things you can do before the test—and that your child can do during the test—to make sure he does as well as he can.

Before the Test

Perhaps the most effective step you can take to prepare your child for standardized tests is to be patient. Remember that no matter how much pressure you put on your child, he won't learn certain skills until he is physically, mentally, and emotionally ready to do so. You've got to walk a delicate line between challenging and

pressuring your child. If you see your child isn't making progress or is getting frustrated, it may be time to lighten up.

Don't Change the Routine. Many experts offer mistaken advice about how to prepare children for a test, such as recommending that children go to bed early the night before or eat a high-protein breakfast on the morning of the test. It's a better idea not to alter your child's routine at all right before the test. If your child isn't used to going to bed early, then sending him off at 7:30 p.m. the night before a test will only make it harder for him to get to sleep by the normal time. If he is used to eating an orange or a piece of toast for breakfast, forcing him to down a platter of fried eggs and bacon will only make him feel sleepy or uncomfortable.

Neatness. Even fourth graders have been known to fill in an answer sheet incorrectly, and unfortunately their errors have made a significant difference on the final test results. Therefore it pays to give your child some practice in filling in answer sheets. Watch how neatly he fills in the bubbles, squares, and rectangles on the following page. If he overlaps the lines, makes a lot of erase marks, or presses the pencil too hard, try having him practice filling in pages of bubbles. You can easily create sheets of capital *O*'s, squares, and rectangles that your child can practice filling in. If he gets bored doing that, have him color in detailed pictures in coloring books, or complete connect-the-dots pages in activity books.

Following Directions. Having good listening skills is crucial to surviving standardized tests. You wouldn't believe how many errors children make because they didn't listen carefully to instructions or didn't pay attention to demonstrations. Some children mark the wrong form, fill in the bubbles incorrectly, or skip to the wrong section. Others simply forget to put their names on the answer sheets. Many children mark the answer sheet without realizing they are marking the wrong bubble.

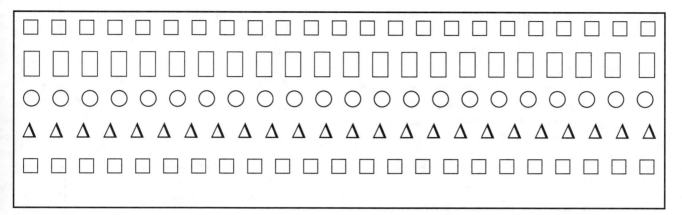

Children need to be reminded that it is important to listen to instructions and to read the directions thoroughly. Each section has its own set of directions, and students need to realize that directions often change from one section to another. Thus students should read all directions very carefully and reread them if they forget what the directions said.

What You and Your Child Can Do

Family Game Night. Playing different games as a family helps your child learn to play games and to follow directions. Every so often introduce a new game, and go through the rules of play together so that everyone understands how to play. This also allows your child to practice interpreting directions.

Homework Drill. Have your child explain the directions for his homework to you to make sure the directions are clear. Encourage him to read the directions carefully and not to miss anything. Go over the directions together for large projects such as book reports.

Science Experiments. Do experiments at home using your child's science textbook, or buy an inexpensive kit at a toy store. There are all kinds of interesting science kits available. This is a productive way to supplement science at home, have some fun, and practice following directions.

Cooking. If there's any activity around the home for which following directions is crucial, it's cooking! Cook at home with your child. Help him to read the recipe and follow along. Baking cookies or cakes or making homemade ice cream or holiday chocolates has a big payoff at the end—your child can eat the results!

Contests. Encourage your child to enter the various contests that exist for children. Writing contests, art contents, poster contests—there's always something happening. A contest is an opportunity for your child to use his talents as well as to gain some practice in reading, interpreting, and following directions (the contest "rules").

Practice Skill: Following Directions

Directions: Read the directions for the writing contest, and answer the questions that follow.

Writing Contest

Sponsored by Authors 'R' Us

The topic for this contest is you: We want you to write your own autobiography. The top three winners will have their stories published in our monthly magazine and receive cash awards, as described in the contest rules. The next five runners up will receive new laptop computers donated by an anonymous company. All entrants will have their names in our magazine and will receive a certificate of participation.

Contest Rules

1.   The author must be between the ages of 8 and 12 years old, and he or she must

have had a twelfth birthday before May 6, 2001.

2. The work must be the entrant's own original work.

3. The essay must be typed, double spaced, and the font size must be 12. There must be 1-inch margins on all sides. The essay should be between two and three pages long.

4. The essay should be typed and submitted on white paper 8½ by 11 inches or mailed electronically to the address below.

5. All entries must be received by noon on April 23, 2002.

6. Entrants may also submit their essays on a disk.

7. The essay is to tell about the author's life so far. It should include his or her earliest years as well as current years.

8. Entrants wishing to receive a list of the winners should send along a self-addressed, stamped envelope with their entries.

9. Each entry should include the author's full name, age, and address, and it should include a statement from his or her parents giving us permission to publish the essay in our magazine.

10. The prizes will be awarded as follows:
    * *Grand prize:* $100 savings bond, having the essay published in our magazine, a new laptop computer, and a certificate of participation
    * *First runner up:* $75 savings bond, having the essay published in our magazine, a new laptop computer, and a certificate of participation
    * *Second runner up:* $50 savings bond, having the essay published in our magazine, a new laptop computer, and a certificate of participation
    * *The next five runners up:* A new laptop computer and a certificate of participation
    * All other entrants will receive a certificate of participation.

11. All winners will be announced on August 18, 2002, and they will be notified by August 21, 2002, by phone.

12. Mail all entries to Authors 'R' Us, 123 Writers Road, East Kalamazoo, WI 54321

Example:

How long should the essay be?

Ⓐ   one to two pages

Ⓑ   two to three pages

Ⓒ   three to four pages

Ⓓ   as long as you want

Answer:

Ⓑ   two to three pages

---

1   How big should the margins be?

Ⓐ   no margins specified

Ⓑ   ½ inch on the sides and 1 inch on the top and bottom

Ⓒ   1-inch margins on all sides

Ⓓ   2 inches on the top and bottom and 1 inch on each side

---

2   Which title would not be appropriate for an essay submitted for this contest?

Ⓐ   My Own Story

Ⓑ   My Life

Ⓒ   The Story of a Girl from Brooklyn

Ⓓ   The Life Habits of a Tasmanian Frog

---

3   Who wins the $100 savings bond?

Ⓐ   grand prize winner

Ⓑ   first runner up

Ⓒ   second runner up

Ⓓ   all entrants

4 When are the entries due?

   (A) May 6, 2002

   (B) April 23, 2002

   (C) August 18, 2002

   (D) May 6, 2001

5 Which format is **not** accepted?

   (A) typed

   (B) disk

   (C) electronic mail

   (D) handwritten

6 What information is **not** required by Authors 'R' Us?

   (A) name

   (B) parent permission

   (C) entrant's school

   (D) age

(See page 109 for answer key.)

During the Test

There are a few other bits of advice to keep in mind that, when followed, have been shown to result in some degree of improvement in a test score. Discuss the following strategies with your child from time to time.

Read the Entire Question First. Some children get so excited about the test that they begin filling in bubbles before they finish reading the entire question. The last few words in a question sometimes give the most important clues to the correct answer. Children should be reminded to be sure to read the entire question—all the way to the end of it—before they try to answer it.

Read All the Answers Carefully. In their desire to finish first, many children tend to select the first answer that seems right to them without thoroughly reading all the responses and choosing the very best answer. Make sure your child understands the importance of evaluating all the answers before choosing one.

Skip Difficult Items the First Time through the Test and Return to Them Later. Many children will sit and worry about a hard question, spending so much time on it that they never get to problems that they would have been able to answer correctly if they only had left enough time. Explain to your child that she can always come back to a knotty question once she finishes the section.

Use Key Words. Have your child look at the questions and try to figure out the parts that are important and those that aren't. Identifying key words is a good way to evaluate questions.

Eliminate Implausible Answer Choices. Just as participants are eliminated in the wildly successful TV show *Who Wants to Be a Millionaire*, remind your child that it's a good idea to narrow down his choices among multiple-choice options by eliminating answers he knows can't possibly be correct.

CHAPTER 2

Vocabulary

The depth and range of a child's vocabulary is a direct outgrowth of her reading ability and the richness and diversity of her environment. Vocabulary continues to develop throughout a child's school years—indeed, dedicated readers never really stop developing and enlarging their language.

What Fourth Graders Should Know

Students in the fourth grade have made the transition from decoding the sounds of the words to knowing the meanings of the words and how to use them effectively in sentences. By this age, teachers are working with students to expand their vocabulary and to write longer and more complicated sentences.

For example, in earlier grades you would expect a student to write a sentence like this: *Our school is big.* In the upper elementary grades, children are expected to write the same sentence more like this: *Our school is large with two floors and three wings.* The key to enabling students to produce these complex sentences is to build their everyday vocabulary so that they can express themselves using a variety of words that express exactly what they want you to understand.

What You and Your Child Can Do

I Spy. This game can be played anywhere, at any time. One person "spies" something and describes it without revealing its identity, as the others guess what it could be. For example, if you spied a painting, your clues might involve words like *rectangular, multicolored, flat, mounted,* or *hand-made.* Alternatively, you can have the guessers ask yes-or-no questions to help them narrow down the choices.

Reading. This is the best activity to build your child's vocabulary. Children who read a variety of materials tend to have a better sense of words and a broader range of vocabulary than those who read only one type of written material. It's typical for children to read every book written about one topic and become expert on the one topic—but they need to read other things as well. Encourage your child to read magazines and newspaper articles and books outside her area.

Password. This classic word game is a great activity for a group of at least four, although you may need to adjust some of the words for your child's reading level.

Crossword Puzzles. Crossword puzzles for children can be lots of fun and challenging, too. They require your child to look for very specific words and require her to use the spelling of other words to narrow the field of choices.

Word of the Day. Make it a family activity to learn a new word each day. Take turns picking the word and introducing it. Everyone tries to use the word at least five times during the day. The family can even have a followup time at dinner to share how family members used the word, or they can have an award for the person who gets the best reaction to using the word (the winner doesn't have to clean up dinner). Keep a list of the words used for the week on the refrigerator so that there are no duplicates.

Wordfind. Here's a popular word game. You can buy whole books of wordfind puzzles that imbed target words amid random letters, requiring a child to search frontward, backward, and sideways to pick out vocabulary words. You can even make up your own wordfind puzzles by scrambling letters around the spelled-out words. While this doesn't address meaning, it does help children with spelling new vocabulary words.

What Tests May Ask

Many standardized tests ask fairly straightforward questions about vocabulary that assess your child's use of language. Tests assess vocabulary by presenting a word and asking children to choose the best definition from among several choices. At this age, your child should be able to make a good guess by eliminating choices that are obviously wrong.

Practice Skill: Vocabulary

Directions: Choose the best definition for the underlined word.

Example:

The new movie is <u>fantastic</u>.

Ⓐ awful

Ⓑ scary

Ⓒ terrific

Ⓓ okay

Answer:

Ⓒ terrific

1 A <u>task</u> is

Ⓐ a place to sleep.

Ⓑ an activity.

Ⓒ a shopping trip.

Ⓓ an animal.

2 <u>Grateful</u> means

Ⓐ angry.

Ⓑ sad.

Ⓒ thankful.

Ⓓ happy.

3 A <u>bargain</u> is

Ⓐ a high-priced item for sale.

Ⓑ a restaurant.

Ⓒ an item for sale at an uncommonly low price.

Ⓓ a loan.

4 An <u>emergency</u> is

Ⓐ an unforeseen circumstance that calls for immediate attention.

Ⓑ a circumstance that can wait to be attended to.

Ⓒ a circumstance that has been expected.

Ⓓ a surprise.

5 A <u>circuit</u> is

Ⓐ a show with horses, acrobats, and clowns.

Ⓑ a wire that carries electricity from one place to another.

Ⓒ a leader of a country.

Ⓓ a type of camera.

6 To <u>gallop</u> means

Ⓐ to run very fast.

Ⓑ a survey of opinions.

Ⓒ to run around the block.

Ⓓ to go to the store.

7 A <u>biscuit</u> is

Ⓐ a dog.

Ⓑ a piece of bread.

Ⓒ a computer.

Ⓓ the end of a book.

8 <u>Monumental</u> means

Ⓐ very small.

Ⓑ statuesque.

Ⓒ carved in stone.

Ⓓ huge.

9 <u>Feisty</u> means

Ⓐ full of energy.

Ⓑ calm.

Ⓒ hungry.

Ⓓ sleepy.

10 To <u>starve</u> is

Ⓐ to go without food.

Ⓑ to have enough food.

Ⓒ to give food to the poor.

Ⓓ to go to a grocery store.

(See page 109 for answer key.)

CHAPTER 3

Word Meanings in Context

In order to read fluently, we must be able to grasp the entire meaning of the combined elements of sentences in a passage, filling in unstated elements almost automatically. This is called *reading words in context,* and it's crucial to a child's ability to understand what he reads.

Words in Context

What Fourth Graders Should Know

Fourth grade is a big year for learning how to use context clues. Students learn how to infer definitions from context clues, and they also learn to use context clues to figure out what is happening in a story. Context clues are used to define the elements of a story and analyze the characters and to help readers predict the outcome. It is a key skill.

What You and Your Child Can Do

Family Book Clubs. Take time as a family to read books together. As you read, discuss the characters of the book. Are they people you would want to meet? What are their interests? How do you know? You can also try to guess what will happen next. If it is a mystery, figure out "whodunit." When you come to a word that may not be familiar, discuss its possible meanings before looking it up in the dictionary. Try to read the sentence before it, the sentence it is in, and the sentence after it to discover its meaning.

Surprises. Plan a surprise for your family and give some clues, and then let the guessing begin.

What Tests May Ask

Standardized tests use context clues to measure a variety of skills. Children need to be able to use the information given to them to find other information that may not be explicit. For example, you can use the information in this sentence to figure out what season it is:

*We wore our **hats, coats, and mittens** to school **to keep warm.***

The clues in the sentence would be the list of clothing and the fact that the children need to keep warm. This information indicates that it is most likely winter.

In order to do well on this type of test, a child should read a passage first, relying on the meaning of the entire sentence in order to help find the answer to specific questions.

Tests may present a sentence and ask a child to define an underlined word, or they may give a brief passage and ask the child to fill in a missing word from a number of possible choices. Tests also may present a passage and then ask questions that require a child to make an educated guess based on verbal clues.

Practice Skill: Word Meanings in Context

Directions: Using context clues, choose the best definition of the underlined word in the question.

Example: The old man couldn't understand the book because he was <u>illiterate</u>.

- (A) happy
- (B) unable to read
- (C) tired
- (D) blind

Answer:

- (B) unable to read

1 The girls <u>screeched</u> loudly when the boys knocked on the window at night.

- (A) whispered
- (B) giggled
- (C) yelled
- (D) talked

2 The stack of newspapers that had accumulated from the last two months was <u>monumental</u>.

- (A) small
- (B) manageable
- (C) slight
- (D) huge

3 Linda wished she had had the <u>forethought</u> to change the outside light bulb before her guests arrived.

- (A) thought ahead of time
- (B) thought after the fact
- (C) thought that originates during sleep
- (D) thought that originates in the forehead

4 We had the best hot and steamy shrimp <u>gumbo</u> before our main course at dinner last night.

- (A) soup
- (B) chewing gum
- (C) boxed shrimp
- (D) bread

5 The cat's <u>keen</u> sense of smell led him straight to the gift of catnip hidden in the closet.

- (A) lousy
- (B) sharp
- (C) bad
- (D) awful

Directions: Read each story below and then choose the best answer to the question that follows it. Make sure you read only one story at a time.

Debbie rushed out the door to school. She was running late and was concentrating only on getting to school. School would start in 5 minutes, and her walk to school would take 10 minutes.

Example:

How late will Debbie be for school?

- (A) 5 minutes
- (B) 10 minutes
- (C) on time
- (D) 15 minutes

Answer:

- (A) 5 minutes

6 Which of these events is most likely to happen next?

ⓐ She runs as fast as she can to get to school.

ⓑ She is on time for school.

ⓒ Her class starts late anyway.

ⓓ Her teacher waits until Debbie arrives before starting the class.

When Debbie arrived, class had already started. As she unpacked her bag, she discovered that she had left her lunch at home. She didn't know what to do. She did not have money to buy lunch, and she didn't really like fish sticks anyway. She would have to come up with a plan before lunch time. She had only had time for a quick breakfast, and she knew she would be starving by lunch.

7 What might Debbie do for her lunch?

ⓐ cook her own

ⓑ ask her friend to share with her

ⓒ steal lunch

ⓓ throw a tantrum

During snack time, Debbie whispered to her friend Carol that she had overslept that morning and had rushed out of the house without her lunch.

"My mom packed me a lunch big enough to feed the whole class!" Carol said. "I'll be glad to share with you."

Debbie gave her friend a big hug and promised to bring a special lunch the next day.

8 How does Debbie probably feel after talking to her friend Carol?

ⓐ grateful   ⓑ mad

ⓒ aggravated   ⓓ indifferent

(See page 109 for answer key.)

Multiple Meanings

Words with more than one meaning must be understood in relation to their context, and they are an important part of a child's vocabulary. Often students don't realize how many words have more than one definition.

What Fourth Graders Should Know

Fourth graders should be aware that words frequently have more than one meaning, and they should be comfortable in picking out the correct meaning by using the context of the sentence to ascertain the definition. Expect your child's teacher to work on multi-meaning words throughout the school year.

What You and Your Child Can Do

Model It. Help your child to understand that words may have multiple meanings. When he asks you for the definition of a word, reply first with the following: "Read the sentence to me first," or "How is it used in the sentence?" These replies help show your child how to discover the context in which a word is used.

Play Family Pun Off. This is a spontaneous activity that can be lots of fun. When someone in your family uses a pun, see if you can continue the conversation using another pun in your next sentence. See how long you can do this.

Read Aloud. Read aloud with your child. When you are reading and come across a word with more than one meaning, stop to take time to discuss the word and what its different meanings are and how to use them. It's also a good idea to ask your child how he knew which definition is appropriate for the particular situation in which the word occurs.

Work through Crossword Puzzles. Crossword puzzles require your child to think about definitions and ideas associated with word meanings. Get a good crossword puzzle book at your child's level, and work on them together. Crossword puzzles can be a good pastime for car rides, and they can be worked on individually or by the family together.

What Tests May Ask

Students are most often asked to use the surrounding sentence or paragraph to decide the definition of multiple-meaning words within actual contexts. To do well on this part of a standardized test, students must consider the entire sentence to decide the meaning of a particular word within it. Standardized tests assess this skill in terms of definitions. The more uses of words your child can identify, the better he will be able to identify them in special contexts.

Practice Skill: Multiple Meanings of Words

Directions: Choose the word or phrase that best defines the underlined word in the question.

Example:

Perdita played an old-fashioned <u>air</u> on the piano.

Ⓐ book

Ⓑ key

Ⓒ song

Ⓓ atmosphere

Answer:

Ⓒ song

9 King Tut was a good <u>ruler</u> of Egypt.

Ⓐ measuring stick

Ⓑ leader

Ⓒ nurse

Ⓓ teacher

10 John put his pet pig away in its <u>pen</u>.

Ⓐ table

Ⓑ bed

Ⓒ writing implement

Ⓓ enclosure

11 The puppy liked to <u>lap</u> his milk.

Ⓐ drink   Ⓑ nudge

Ⓒ cuddle   Ⓓ eat

12 I cut my <u>palm</u> and bruised two fingers when I shut my hand in the car door.

Ⓐ a tropical tree

Ⓑ a part of the hand

Ⓒ the lower part of the leg

Ⓓ the elbow

Directions: Choose the word that best fits in the blanks of both sentences.

13 Last night Jared built a big ____ at the campsite.

The boss will ____ his workers if they don't do a good job.

Ⓐ plant   Ⓑ fire

Ⓒ tent   Ⓓ hire

14 We have to ____ up to what we've done.

Peaches is going to wash her ____.

Ⓐ face

Ⓑ hear

Ⓒ eyes

Ⓓ head

15 Our car swerved when we got a hole in our ____.

Suki says she will never ____ of reading.

(A) window

(B) door

(C) like

(D) tire

---

16 Chandra likes to ____ her nails.

The secretary will ____ the letter in the cabinet.

(A) paint

(B) file

(C) lose

(D) put

17 If you play the piano, you need to have short ____.

Juan used a lot of ____ to build his club-house.

(A) hair

(B) wood

(C) nails

(D) legs

---

18 Will you ____ the door?

I can smell smoke, so the fire must be ____ by.

(A) open

(B) near

(C) shut

(D) close

(See page 109 for answer key.)

CHAPTER 4

Synonyms, Antonyms, and Homophones

Understanding the concepts of "alike" and "different" is very important to the development of reading comprehension. Thus recognizing synonyms, antonyms, and homophones is a skill children need to develop along with their reading and writing skills.

Synonyms and Antonyms

Skillful use of synonyms and antonyms can help make stories and compositions more colorful and exciting. Teachers therefore often work with words as they relate to other words as a way to help students more accurately describe their stories. Synonyms and antonyms are also useful tools for learning vocabulary words. When students practice their vocabulary words, they are often asked to find synonyms or antonyms.

What Fourth Graders Should Know

Fourth graders readily understand that two different words can mean the same or opposite thing, and most are comfortable with the terms *synonym* and *antonym*. Because your fourth grader probably understands abstract and complex terms quite well, she'll be able to easily identify many synonyms and antonyms for abstract words. For example, your child should understand that *beautiful* and *gorgeous* mean the same thing.

In contrast to younger children who insisted that *purse* and *pocketbook* are different things, your fourth grader can grasp the idea that these two words refer to the same object. Moreover,

they fully comprehend one-way relationships; that is, that while all dachshunds are dogs, not all dogs are dachshunds.

What You and Your Child Can Do

Word of the Week. Here's a fun family activity that's sure to get the competitive juices flowing. Each participant commits to learning a new word each week and posts it on the refrigerator. During the course of the week, players should add as many synonyms and antonyms for the word as they can find. New words should be used in daily conversations and writing.

Top It! Here's a game many fourth graders just love and that works well on long car rides:

CHILD: I'm cute.

YOU: I'm pretty!

CHILD: I'm gorgeous!

YOU: I'm ravishing!

The game continues until no one can think of any more synonyms for the one word. Then you can begin all over again with new words.

Crossword Puzzles. Crossword puzzles related to topics in which students are interested or are studying in school are fun and help students think about synonyms and antonyms. The nature of these puzzles also help students to really brainstorm different possibilities.

Word Storm. Here's a good family game for a stormy night when everyone's gathered together at home. Using a dictionary, one player chooses a word. Give the definition of the word and make sure that everyone understands its meaning. Then, using a stopwatch or egg timer, everyone has one to three minutes to write as many synonyms or antonyms as they can think of for that word. At the end of the designated time, everyone compares lists. The winner is the one with the most words.

Synonym Picture Game. Here's another family game that encourages children to think in terms of synonyms and antonyms. Using one large sheet of drawing paper, everyone gathers around to play. The player who is "it" announces she's looking for a word that means "big." Then she begins to draw simple pictures to represent the synonym she has in mind. Looking at her drawing, the other family members try to guess the word she has in mind. If her word is *big* and the synonym she has in mind is *gigantic,* she might draw a huge whale next to a tiny boat. The first person to correctly guess her word is then it.

What Tests May Ask

Standardized testing for the fourth grade will use different methods to assess your child's understanding of words in relation to their antonyms and synonyms. Your child may be asked to choose a synonym or antonym from among a group of choices. Some tests may list pairs of words and ask in which pair do the words mean the same (or opposite).

Practice Skill: Synonyms

Directions: Choose the best synonym for each word underlined in the question.

Example:

I like to play by the <u>ocean</u>.

- (A) lake
- (B) river
- (C) pond
- (D) sea

Answer:

- (D) sea

---

1 It is important to follow the <u>rules</u>.
- (A) laws
- (B) judgments
- (C) customary manners
- (D) fools

---

2 There was such <u>excitement</u> at the start of the Olympics!
- (A) sadness
- (B) depression
- (C) strong enthusiasm
- (D) boredom

---

3 The boat was going to <u>drift</u> out to sea.
- (A) run
- (B) walk
- (C) wander
- (D) float

---

4 Carl's grandmother was an <u>elderly</u> woman.
- (A) young
- (B) old
- (C) rocky
- (D) dark

---

5 The two sides of the team were <u>equal</u> in ability.
- (A) same
- (B) unfair
- (C) larger
- (D) smaller

(See page 109 for the answer key.)

Practice Skill: Antonyms

Directions: Choose the word with the opposite meaning of the given word in the question.

Example:

extinguish

- (A) ignite
- (B) blot
- (C) blow out
- (D) stir up

Answer:

- (A) ignite

---

6 polite

- (A) courteous
- (B) kind
- (C) thoughtful
- (D) rude

---

7 gloomy

- (A) dark
- (B) sad
- (C) happy
- (D) distant

---

8 huge

- (A) large
- (B) tiny
- (C) huge
- (D) medium

---

9 separate

- (A) join
- (B) distant
- (C) away
- (D) opposite

---

10 float

- (A) sink
- (B) drift
- (C) sail
- (D) wander

(See page 109 for the answer key.)

Homophones

Homophones can be a child's biggest spelling challenge, but she needs to master them nevertheless. Learning these words is an ongoing process in your child's education; it's a skill that requires your child to visualize words as well as hear and speak them. At the same time, homophones can be lots of fun, and many children really enjoy working with them.

The terms *homophone* and *homonym* are often used interchangeably, but their meanings are slightly different. *Homophones* are words that are pronounced the same but are spelled differently (such as *heir* and *air*) or used to convey different meanings. *Homonyms* are words that are both spelled and pronounced the same, but they can be used to convey different meanings. For example, *coat* can be a verb ("The chocolate coats the apple") or a noun ("Please put on your coat"). Note that all homonyms are also homophones.

What Fourth Graders Should Know

Younger children can be quite inflexible with homophones and insist that *head* means what's on your shoulders and cannot possibly also mean "the leader of a group." However, by fourth grade children are able to understand the subtleties of multi-meaning words. They understand that a word can have multiple meanings, and most really enjoy coming up with homophones and homonyms.

What You and Your Child Can Do

Newspaper Search. Here's a fun activity to do when your family is finished reading the newspaper. Pick an article appropriate for your child's age and have her identify as many homophones in the article as she can find. Add to the fun by using shapes—for example, trace a large heart shape on the newspaper and cut it out. Use the articles in that area as the "search field" for homophones.

Homonym Hunt. Send two children on a homonym scavenger hunt, searching for items (for example, in your kitchen) that have a second meaning: the "batter" in your mixing bowl and a "batter" in a baseball game, the "bowl" on your shelf and the verb meaning "to bowl," the "fork" in the drawer and a "fork" in the road. Have your child make a list of these words and keep it on the fridge. See how long the list can get.

Write a Story. *Amelia Bedelia* is a classic children's book series filled with wonderful homophones that kids just love. Your child may already have read a book or two in this series. If so, have your child write a story of several paragraphs' length with a main character like Amelia, using at least five homophones. After she writes the paragraphs, have her draw a picture of the homophone pairs.

Practice Skill: Homophones

Directions: Choose the correct word to complete each sentence.

Example:

We met at the picnic _____ for lunch.

(A) cite

(B) site

(C) sight

(D) cit

Answer:

(B) site

---

11 Lindsay and Colleen took _____ project to the state competition.

(A) they're

(B) their

(C) there

(D) they are

---

12 Miss Callahan took her class to the science _____ at Harvard University.

(A) fair

(B) fare

(C) faire

(D) fayre

---

13 Justin convinced his mother to buy him a new computer because there was a big _____.

Ⓐ sail

Ⓑ sale

Ⓒ sayle

Ⓓ saile

14 Actors often tell each other to "_____ a leg" before a big show to wish them good luck.

Ⓐ brake

Ⓑ break

Ⓒ brak

Ⓓ brakie

15 Juan's dad ordered a big _____ for dinner tonight at the restaurant.

Ⓐ steak

Ⓑ stake

Ⓒ stak

Ⓓ steek

16 Sonya forgot to moisten the _____ for her clarinet before she began to practice.

Ⓐ read

Ⓑ reed

Ⓒ reade

Ⓓ reede

17 Jenny had to measure her _____ before she could buy a pattern for her new skirt.

Ⓐ waste

Ⓑ waist

Ⓒ waiste

Ⓓ wast

18 Last night we went to the movies and decided to _____ a large box of popcorn.

Ⓐ bye

Ⓑ by

Ⓒ buy

Ⓓ not given

19 Amanda and Laura played games on the computer for one _____.

Ⓐ are

Ⓑ our

Ⓒ hour

Ⓓ oure

20 At the end of the day, Mother told Megan to throw her clothes down the laundry _____.

Ⓐ chut

Ⓑ shoot

Ⓒ chuet

Ⓓ chute

(See page 109 for the answer key.)

CHAPTER 5

Spelling

A student's ability to "dissect" words to determine their spelling and meaning is a key to becoming a better reader—and also to doing well on most standardized tests. In fourth grade, students are challenged to discover the meaning of unfamiliar words, verify spelling, and use words correctly. This section will help you work with your child to help him understand various ways we work with words.

Root Words

A *root word* (also called *base word*) is the original form of a word that can be made into another word by adding a prefix or suffix. For example, the root word in *brightest* is *bright*.

What Fourth Graders Should Know

Students in the fourth grade should be able to identify the base, or root, word of words with different common endings such as *-ing, -ed,* and *-es.* Part of being able to do this is also being able to recognize and use all spelling rules, including irregular spellings.

For example, if the given word is *happiness,* the student needs to recognize the base word as *happy* and not *happi.* It's also necessary for fourth graders to be able to add endings to words and create the correct meaning and spelling.

The key spelling rules fourth graders need to know how to use are listed below.

1. **Words ending in *-z, -s, -x, -ch, -ve, -sh,* and *-ss*** are made plural by adding *-es.* For example, *fox* becomes *foxes, dress* becomes *dresses,* and *wish* becomes *wishes.*

2. **Words that end in a consonant followed by *-y*** are made plural by changing the *-y* to *-i* and adding *-es.* For example, *family* becomes *families.*

3. **Many of the words ending in *-f* and *-fe*** are made plural by changing the *-f* to a *-v* and adding *-es.* For example, *loaf* becomes *loaves.*

4. **To add a suffix to a word,** the final consonant is doubled if the word meets one of the following requirements:

   - It is a one-syllable word and ends with a single consonant other than *-x.* For example, *pet* becomes *petting.*

   - When the final accent syllable ends in a single consonant (other than *-x*) preceded by a single vowel. For example, *begin* becomes *beginning.*

5. **When a word ends in *-ll*** and the suffix to be added is *-ly,* drop the final *-l* and add *-ly.* For example, *full* becomes *fully.*

What You and Your Child Can Do

Home Publishing Company. Start your own publishing house! Have each member of your family sit down and write his or her own biography. If you have a computer, let everyone take turns to print out a copy. Add colorful covers or binders—and add your own art! Then take turns sharing what you've created. While you do this, check your child's spelling. Don't be harsh, but gently point out errors. Most kids love "spellcheck" features in word processing software, and having the computer check spelling can be a painless way to work on this skill. But remember: If your child writes on a computer, make sure he checks his own spelling before using the computer's spellcheck.

If your child likes this activity, branch out. Have him write and illustrate his own stories. Today's computer programs can really add some fun graphics or art. Or have your child create a family newspaper, which you can then mail off in a holiday card or send it round to farflung family members.

Letter Writing. Writing letters and thank you notes to relatives and friends isn't just good manners—it will also help your child think about writing and spelling words correctly. Make sure he proofreads for accuracy. If a word is spelled incorrectly, make sure he corrects it before sending off the letter.

Family Game Night. Your family can make learning fun by playing games as a family. Playing games like *Scrabble* and hangman can build a sense of words as well as create some fun family time.

What Tests May Ask

You can be sure that standardized tests for the fourth grade will include questions on root words. In some cases, students will be asked to identify the root word from a group of given words. Some will be straightforward, such as knowing the root word of *playing,* but some may be more difficult, such as understanding that *house* is the root word for *housing* even though the *e* has been dropped. Tests also may ask your child to choose from given pairs of words the pair that shares the same root word.

Practice Skill: Root Words

Directions: Choose the base word for each of the given words.

Example:

mistreated

- Ⓐ mis
- Ⓑ ed
- Ⓒ treat
- Ⓓ treated

Answer:

- Ⓒ treat

---

1 compacted
- Ⓐ com
- Ⓑ pacted
- Ⓒ compact
- Ⓓ pact

---

2 families
- Ⓐ family
- Ⓑ famine
- Ⓒ fam
- Ⓓ mily

---

3 loved
- Ⓐ lov
- Ⓑ love
- Ⓒ loved
- Ⓓ lovely

---

4 childish

   (A) childish

   (B) child

   (C) ish

   (D) children

5 reddened

   (A) dened

   (B) ed

   (C) red

   (D) redd

Directions: Choose the pair of words in which the base word is the same.

Example:

   (A) inactive—activate

   (B) ran—ranted

   (C) hopeful—fully

   (D) vocal—voice

Answer:

   (A) inactive—activate

6 (A) unlawful—lawfully

   (B) pieced—peaceable

   (C) together—getting

   (D) awful—fully

7 (A) pizzazz—pizzas

   (B) peace—peas

   (C) footing—fooling

   (D) started—starting

Directions: Choose the correctly spelled word.

Example:

   (A) reindeers

   (B) spoked

   (C) runing

   (D) cautious

Answer:

   (D) cautious

8 (A) happyly

   (B) happiness

   (C) happenning

   (D) happie

9 (A) calfs

   (B) leafes

   (C) knives

   (D) wolfs

10 (A) sofaes

   (B) nutts

   (C) tomatos

   (D) telephoned

(See page 109 for the answer key.)

Prefixes and Suffixes

Discovering the meaning of unknown words is a skill that everyone uses throughout life. One of the keys to being able to puzzle out words easily lies in knowing what the different suffixes and prefixes are and what they mean.

What Fourth Graders Should Know

In fourth grade, children learn more complex rules regarding suffixes and prefixes. The list of suffixes and prefixes is lengthy, but some common suffixes and prefixes that fourth graders should know (together with their meanings) are listed below:

Prefixes

pre-: meaning "before" (*precaution*)

post-: meaning "after" (*postpone, postdate*)

un-: meaning "not" (*unhappy, uncomfortable*)

mid-: meaning "middle" (*midnight, midyear*)

mis-: meaning "wrong" or "not" (*mistake, miscount*)

ex:- meaning "former" (*ex-president, ex-student*)

in- or *im-:* meaning "not" (*incorrect, imperfect*)

Suffixes

-ology: meaning "study of" (*biology,* the study of life science)

-ist: meaning "one who practices something particular" (*pharmacist*)

-ic: meaning "relating to" (*historic, poetic*)

-able: meaning "is" or "can be" (*comfortable, climbable*)

-est: meaning "most" (*smartest, smallest*)

-ify: meaning "to make" (*beautify, falsify*)

-en: meaning "to make" (*strengthen, soften*)

What You and Your Child Can Do

Family Game Night. Everyone in your family can learn new words and practice by playing games together. The following games will increase your family's use of words and spelling of words: *Scrabble, Upwords, Password,* and *Boggle.*

Newspaper Search. Pick an article in the newspaper that is appropriate for your child to read and have him see how many words he can find with prefixes or suffixes. This also works well using articles from your child's favorite magazines.

Word Searches and Crossword Puzzles. Both of these games can provide great opportunities for children to expand their vocabularies and their spelling skills.

Go Fish! Here's a great game for two or more players! Make up a set of 3×5 index cards, half with various prefixes and suffixes (such as *un-, mis-, -ing, -ed,* or *-s,* half with simple root words (such as *play, run, jump*). Deal out five cards to each player (the leftover cards are for "fishing"). The youngest player begins, asking one of the other players for an "ending" or "root" card to match one of his cards to make a pair—a pair is a prefix or suffix that could match with a root word. For example, if the player has the root word *play,* he could ask for a suffix *-ing* to form *playing.*

If the other player has the card, he must hand it over. The first player asks for another match until he's turned down. If the player being asked doesn't have the card, he says "Go fish!" The other person then must pick up a card from the go fish pile. Each of the pairs is placed down as they are matched. When a player runs out of cards, the pairs are counted, and the one with the most pairs wins.

Memory. This is a fun game in which you make up sets of cards with different types of pairs such as a prefix and a root word with the prefix; a suffix, and the root word; a sentence with a missing word and the missing word, and synonyms and antonyms using words with prefixes (*correct* and *incorrect*). The cards are placed face down and mixed up. A player takes his turn by flipping over two cards. If the cards match, he keeps the pair. If they don't match, the cards are flipped back over and the next person takes a turn. When all of the matches have been found, the pairs are counted, and the player with the most pairs wins.

Practice Skill: Prefixes and Suffixes

Directions: Choose the word that best completes the sentence.

Example:

He was the best baseball _____ the coach had ever seen.

(A) glove

(B) player

(C) playor

(D) play

Answer:

(B) player

11 Carolyn went to see a heart _____ to find out if she needed an operation.

(A) nurse

(B) teacher

(C) specialist

(D) thinker

12 James took the butter out of the freezer to _____ it.

(A) soften

(B) softer

(C) softest

(D) harden

13 Lucky was the _____ dog we have ever had.

(A) smarter

(B) smartest

(C) smart

(D) smartable

14 Dennis's favorite subject is _____, the study of life science.

(A) history

(B) physics

(C) biology

(D) musicology

15 Did you take our guests on a tour of the Old Parker Tavern, an _____ restored home?

(A) artistic

(B) historic

(C) panoramic

(D) physic

Directions: Choose the word that best fits the given definition.

Example:

someone who works in the field of chemistry

(A) biologist

(B) chemist

(C) chemical

(D) chemistry

Answer:

(B) chemist

16 someone who specializes in hair styling

(A) styling (B) styled

(C) stylist (D) stylistic

17 to pay before

    Ⓐ repay

    Ⓑ payable

    Ⓒ paid

    Ⓓ prepay

18 middle of the ship

    Ⓐ shipped

    Ⓑ shipping

    Ⓒ shipable

    Ⓓ midship

19 not perfect

    Ⓐ imperfect

    Ⓑ inperfect

    Ⓒ unperfect

    Ⓓ misperfect

20 not understood

    Ⓐ ununderstood

    Ⓑ disunderstood

    Ⓒ misunderstood

    Ⓓ understood

(See page 109 for the answer key.)

Singular and Plural

The rules for adding endings to words include the correct way to make the plural forms of verbs and nouns and the correct way to make them agree (the *dog runs,* the *dogs run*). Knowing the correct forms of plural and singular words is one of the most important parts of learning how to express your thoughts correctly.

What Fourth Graders Should Know

Students in the fourth grade should be able to spell and identify singular and plural nouns, as well as to implement the rules for correct subject-verb agreement. For fourth graders, the subject-verb agreement tends to be the most challenging skill that must be mastered during the year.

Most students can tell you if a noun is singular or plural, but verbs are a challenge all by themselves. Most adults make this agreement automatically and don't think about it, but it doesn't come quite so easily to children.

In addition, children in the fourth grade are expected to recognize a noun whose spelling changes to make it plural, such as:

goose—geese

mouse—mice

child—children

tooth—teeth

Some words don't change from singular to plural. Some of the most common that fourth graders may come across include the following:

moose

dozen

deer

fish

traffic

The general rule for making a noun plural is to add *-s* or *-es* to the word. The rule for making a verb plural in the present tense is to take away the *s*. Of course, there are exceptions to every rule. However, here are some examples that conform to the rule:

Singular

Sonya's dog jumps with delight when she gets home from school.

Danielle hopes to go to Renee's birthday party.

His dog Smokey runs into the house every time a thunderstorm starts.

Plural

The dogs jump at the door to scare away robbers.

Michael, Matt, and Gus hope Miss Bowles won't give them a lot of homework.

Whiskers and Snoopy like to watch birds from the window.

What You and Your Child Can Do

Word of the Day. If your family is learning a new word each day, part of that time can be spent practicing using the words in sentences. Keeping an ongoing list of the words and using them for review will help your child become a better writer as well as help him answer these types of questions in standardized tests. List both the singular and plural forms of the word, if applicable.

Proofreading. Take time to help your child to check over his homework for proper spelling and use of plural words. If a word is used incorrectly, have him read it out loud to make sure it sounds right. You'll be surprised how easy it can be for your child to "hear" something is wrong that he may not notice just by reading silently.

Spelling Words. Expand the use of the spelling words by making them plural or singular. Practicing spelling words using a variety of textures will help cement the different spellings in your child's memory. Here are some practical and fun ways to do this:

• Use magnetic letters on the refrigerator or a cookie sheet.

• Sprinkle salt or sugar on a baking sheet and trace the words.

• Write the words with your index finger on a piece of textured fabric or sandpaper.

• Write the words in whipped cream or shaving cream.

• Write the words on your child's back and have him guess the words you write.

What Tests May Ask

Standardized tests for fourth graders may assess plural and singular knowledge by presenting sentences and asking students to fill in the blank with the correctly spelled word. At this age, the tests will probably focus on words that are irregular that fourth graders should be expected to be able to spell correctly.

Practice Skill: Singular and Plural

Directions: Choose the word that best completes the sentence.

Example:

We have to rake the _____.

Ⓐ leafs

Ⓑ lavs

Ⓒ leafes

Ⓓ leaves

Answer:

Ⓓ leaves

---

21 Miss Cook brought six _____ to the picnic on Saturday.

Ⓐ student

Ⓑ studentes

Ⓒ studentss

Ⓓ students

---

22 The girls _____ six miles every day after school.

Ⓐ runs

Ⓑ rans

Ⓒ run

Ⓓ runned

---

23 Dianne and Elaine _____ the boys to the park each week.

Ⓐ bring

Ⓑ brings

Ⓒ brunged

Ⓓ broughts

24 The girls _____ at the mall each week after skating.

Ⓐ shops

Ⓑ shopes

Ⓒ shop

Ⓓ shopss

25 Eric _____ houses on the weekends.

Ⓐ paints

Ⓑ paintes

Ⓒ paint

Ⓓ paints'

26 The _____ chases mice in the field.

Ⓐ cats

Ⓑ cates

Ⓒ catss

Ⓓ cat

27 _____ draw pictures of the planets.

Ⓐ The boys

Ⓑ Billy

Ⓒ The boy

Ⓓ The boy's

28 Gus and Dan saw six _____ on the side of the road.

Ⓐ mooses

Ⓑ moose

Ⓒ meese

Ⓓ meeses

29 There is a _____ on each corner of the street.

Ⓐ church

Ⓑ churches

Ⓒ churchs

Ⓓ churchez

30 How many _____ are in the fourth-grade class?

Ⓐ child

Ⓑ childs

Ⓒ children

Ⓓ childrens

(See page 109 for the answer key.)

Compound Words

Compound words are created by combining two or more smaller words into one. Students need to remember that when a word becomes a part of a compound word, it may not retain its original definition.

What Fourth Graders Should Know

In the fourth grade, students are refining their ability to spell and create compound words. Students in fourth grade should be able to easily recognize compound words.

What You and Your Child Can Do

Word Families. Pick a word to see how many compound words your child can make with the word. For example, choose the word *fire* and have your child list as many words as he can that include the word *fire*. The list may look something like this:

> fireplace
>
> firelight
>
> fireworks
>
> firewood
>
> firefighter
>
> fireproof

Puzzles. Write a variety of compound words on strips of paper or oaktag. Cut the words apart using crooked lines, like a puzzle piece. Have your child match the words up. The activity can be extended by having your child use the words in sentences or find other words he can match up to make new words.

Fridge Magnets. Have your child make up compound words using refrigerator magnet letters. If you'd rather make your own magnets, you can buy sheets of magnetic paper at your local office supply store. Using your computer, compose a list of words that can be made into compound words, and print them out on the magnetic paper (or just write them down yourself on the paper). Cut them apart.

Now that you have a list of words to use, put them on the refrigerator and pair them to make the compound words. See if someone else in the family can change just one word to make a new compound word. For example, start with *basketball*. The next person may change it to *football*. *Football* may then be changed to *footwear*, and so on. See how long you can keep this up!

Board Games. There are a variety of commercial board games that help with compound words, including *Scrabble, Pictionary, Boggle* (and *Boggle Junior*), and *Upwords*.

Newspaper or Book Searches. Have your child search for compound words in articles in newspapers or magazines. If he doesn't know the meaning of a word, have him look it up in a dictionary.

I Spy. While taking a long drive or waiting in a long line, see if you can "spy" things whose names are compound words. For example, if you were waiting to get into the movies, you'd see *popcorn*.

Compound Word Charades. Play a game of charades using only compound words.

What Tests May Ask

Standardized tests in fourth grade may include a few questions about compound words, usually asking students to choose the compound word from a group of choices or to choose the correct definition of a compound word.

Practice Skill: Compound Words

Directions: Choose the best definition for the underlined word in the question.

Example:

> We made a <u>scarecrow</u> for the garden.
>
> (A) a funny doll
>
> (B) a stuffed figure to frighten away birds in a garden
>
> (C) a stuffed crow to scare cats
>
> (D) a stuffed crow to scare snakes

Answer:

> (B) a stuffed figure to frighten away birds in a garden

31 The families shared a school <u>carpool</u> for rainy days.

    Ⓐ   a way to share rides to one place

    Ⓑ   a car with a pool in the back

    Ⓒ   a pool in the shape of a car

    Ⓓ   a table with pockets in the shape of a car

32 The boys went to the <u>baseball</u> game.

    Ⓐ   alone   Ⓑ   separately

    Ⓒ   in a group   Ⓓ   not given

33 David's picture was on the front of the <u>newspaper</u>.

    Ⓐ   a new paper

    Ⓑ   the newest kind of paper

    Ⓒ   a periodical that tells of events

    Ⓓ   a kind of TV show

34 Mother bought a new <u>lampshade</u>.

    Ⓐ   a shaded lamp

    Ⓑ   a lamp with a shade

    Ⓒ   a lamp in the dark

    Ⓓ   a covering for a lamp

35 Stu, Nathan, Joel, and Ian play <u>basketball</u> each week.

    Ⓐ   a basket for storing balls

    Ⓑ   a sport with a hoop and ball

    Ⓒ   a ball that looks like a basket

    Ⓓ   a basket shaped like ball

(See page 109 for the answer key.)

Contractions

A *contraction* is a shortened form of two combined words in which the words maintain their meanings. One word keeps its spelling, and the other is a shortened spelling. The words are joined using an apostrophe. Contractions are used to combine a pronoun and a verb (*I* + *will* = *I'll*) or a verb and the adverb *not* (*does* + *not* = *doesn't*).

What Fourth Graders Should Know

By fourth grade, students should have mastered contractions. At this age, the challenge lies in understanding that contractions are also homophones. In particular, students seem to struggle with *their, they're,* and *there,* and with understanding when to use the contraction *it's* and when to use the pronoun showing possession, *its.*

What You and Your Child Can Do

Newspaper or Book Search. Have your child look through articles or books and circle all the contractions on a page. To make it more challenging, set a timer and have a contest between at least two players.

Contraction Race. Set an egg timer and see who can list the most correctly spelled contractions.

Being an Editor. Write a story for your child in which you spell out all words. Then challenge him to change all of the more formal words into contractions.

Practice Skill: Contractions

Directions: Select the correct contraction for the underlined words in the question.

Example:

He <u>is not</u> going to school today.

    Ⓐ   i'snt   Ⓑ   is'nt

    Ⓒ   isn't   Ⓓ   isnt'

Answer:

   Ⓒ isn't

---

36 Joseph <u>was not</u> at the park today.

   Ⓐ was'not

   Ⓑ wasn't

   Ⓒ wa'not

   Ⓓ wasnt'

---

37 <u>They are</u> going to Mrs. Driscoll's office.

   Ⓐ They're

   Ⓑ There

   Ⓒ The're

   Ⓓ They'are

---

38 <u>It is</u> Missy's birthday!

   Ⓐ Its

   Ⓑ Its'

   Ⓒ It's

   Ⓓ Itis'

---

39 <u>I will</u> take you to the movies.

   Ⓐ I'l

   Ⓑ I'ld

   Ⓒ I'll

   Ⓓ Ill

---

40 Caitlin <u>will not</u> be able to attend the spelling bee.

   Ⓐ won't

   Ⓑ willn't

   Ⓒ wiln't

   Ⓓ willnt'

---

41 Lauren <u>should have</u> won the writing contest.

   Ⓐ should'v

   Ⓑ should'ave

   Ⓒ should've

   Ⓓ shouldve'

---

42 Sally <u>does not</u> have Susie's new e-mail address.

   Ⓐ dosen't

   Ⓑ doesn't

   Ⓒ dosent'

   Ⓓ does't

---

43 K. C. <u>would not</u> let Luke feed the goats.

   Ⓐ wouldnt'

   Ⓑ wouldn't

   Ⓒ woul'not

   Ⓓ wouldnt

44 Mom <u>has not</u> gone to the grocery store this week.

(A) hasnt

(B) has'not

(C) has't

(D) hasn't

45 The leaves on the trees <u>are not</u> changing colors.

(A) arn't

(B) aren't

(C) aren'ot

(D) aren'tt

(See page 109 for the answer key.)

CHAPTER 6

Grammar

Capable readers and fluent writers need to understand and use the appropriate grammar rules, including the regular and irregular use of nouns, pronouns, verbs, and adjectives.

Parts of Speech

What Fourth Graders Should Know

By fourth grade, children have learned to generalize the rules of the English language and understand the concept of both regular and irregular tenses. Children can understand what pronouns are (including masculine and feminine pronouns, plural pronouns, and neutral pronouns) and how to make them possessive.

Fourth graders continue to work on verbs and tenses, and they know that many verbs don't follow regular rules. In addition, their grasp of written expression has developed to the point where they can judge when simple sentences are formed correctly. By fourth grade, your child should be comfortable with adjectives and their comparative forms, including the irregular forms (if one piece of candy is *good,* two is *better,* and five is the *best*).

What You and Your Child Can Do

Read! Your child may be in the fourth grade, but that doesn't mean you should stop reading together. Reading a wide variety of books is one of the best ways to teach grammar—simply reading good examples of the English language will do a lot to help expose your child to correct forms of English.

Listen. Reading isn't the only way to reinforce the language—your child's hearing you use it correctly when you talk is also fundamentally important. Remember that it will be much easier for your child to learn proper grammar in the beginning than to have to unlearn sloppy language habits. If you've modeled correct grammar from early childhood, the correct words will just come naturally to your child.

Play Computer Games. Learning can be fun, and no one knows that better than the producers of kids' computer games. Many computer games currently on the market can help boost good grammar skills in such fun ways your child won't even notice she's learning. *Kid Works Deluxe* (Davidson) encourages youngsters to create multimedia books, stories, poems, and more using words together with pictures and sounds. In *Grammar Games* (Davidson), children can participate in rain forest activities as they solve problems of plurals and possessives, identify subject-verb agreements, edit sentences for proper verb usage, and recognize sentence fragments. The game includes a complete grammar guide that provides grammar rules and examples at the click of the mouse.

Write *Mad Libs.* Everyone in fourth grade loves *Mad Libs* books. These inexpensive paperback workbooks offer a story with blanks asking your child to list a noun, verb, or adjective. When the child then inserts these random parts of speech into the story, the result can be screamingly funny. But you don't need to buy commercial varieties of these games—your child can make her own!

Have her write a brief story, leaving blanks in crucial spots where words are left out. Another player can fill in the blanks with adjectives, nouns, verbs, or pronouns. Then your child can read the story with the other player's words in the blanks. For example, here's a story with blanks that your child might write:

One day the NOUN jumped into his ADJECTIVE convertible NOUN and drove off with his ADJECTIVE NOUN.

The other player might offer these words:

noun: cat

adjective: furry

noun: banana

adjective: scraggly

noun: suspenders

Your child would then read the completed story:

One day the CAT jumped into his FURRY convertible BANANA and drove off with his SCRAGGLY SUSPENDERS.

Build a Story. This can be lots of fun for kids spending the night together. Have one child start off writing a story (the children can use a computer or write the story by hand). After a few sentences (preferably in an exciting part), one child stops the story and the next child begins. Then the third child picks up the tale, and so on. Have them pay special attention to parts of speech as they work on the story.

Write a Letter. Since the best way to practice grammar is simply to practice writing, anything you can do to get your child to write will help.

Suggest that she might like to send a brief note to her favorite author or illustrator, explaining why she likes a particular book. Check over grammar and usage and make gentle corrections, if necessary.

What Tests May Ask

The usual way to find out how well a child understands grammar is to assign essays and ask children to provide short answers to questions. While this is effective in the classroom, most standardized tests today still find it most practical to assess grammar skills by testing a child's ability to *recognize* correct usage. On this type of test, a child must read a sentence and then choose the correct answer for the blank.

Because recognizing correct usage is much easier than trying to come up with the correct part of speech or usage on her own, a few states are trying to include a writing sample as part of the test. However, most states still do not offer this choice, and most standardized tests therefore continue to use multiple-choice questions.

Practice Skill: Nouns

Directions: Read the following sentences and choose the correct noun to go in the blank.

Example:

There was one goose sitting by the pond. Three _____ went flying overhead.

(A) goose

(B) gooses

(C) geese

(D) geeses

Answer:

(C) geese

1 Do you have _____ backpack?

   Ⓐ Mels

   Ⓑ Mel's

   Ⓒ Mels'

   Ⓓ Mel

2 Both _____ will be in school today.

   Ⓐ twins

   Ⓑ twins'

   Ⓒ twin's

   Ⓓ twin

(See page 109 for the answer key.)

Practice Skill: Verbs

Directions: Read each sentence and choose the letter underneath the verb.

Example:

She ran to the store.
Ⓐ Ⓑ   Ⓒ   Ⓓ

   Ⓐ She

   Ⓑ ran

   Ⓒ the

   Ⓓ store

Answer:

   Ⓑ ran

3 Sue jumped down from her horse.
Ⓐ   Ⓑ   Ⓒ Ⓓ

   Ⓐ Sue   Ⓑ jumped

   Ⓒ her   Ⓓ horse

4 Mandy and Tom decided not to come.
   Ⓐ   Ⓑ   Ⓒ Ⓓ

   Ⓐ Mandy

   Ⓑ decided

   Ⓒ not

   Ⓓ to

(See page 109 for the answer key.)

Practice Skill: Pronouns

Directions: Read the sentences below and choose the correct pronoun to go in the blank.

Example:

Sharon hung up _____ clothes.

   Ⓐ her

   Ⓑ she

   Ⓒ hers

   Ⓓ it

Answer:

   Ⓐ her

5 Peter ran to get _____ coat and hat.

   Ⓐ him   Ⓑ he

   Ⓒ his   Ⓓ she

6 The dog lay down on _____ bed.

   Ⓐ he   Ⓑ she

   Ⓒ hers   Ⓓ its

(See page 109 for the answer key.)

Practice Skill: Adjectives

Directions: Choose the sentence that is written correctly.

Example:

   (A) I like chocolate, but I like vanilla better.

   (B) Of all the books, Sam liked that one good.

   (C) That dress is more better than this one.

   (D) It's the bestest game we've had!

Answer:

   (A) I like chocolate, but I like vanilla better.

---

7 (A) This is the worstest day of my life.

   (B) Math may be hard, but chemistry is even harder.

   (C) Yesterday it was hottest than two weeks ago.

   (D) Tomorrow it was the hottest day we've had.

(See page 110 for the answer key.)

Punctuation

Whether it's commas, periods, quotation marks, or exclamation points, punctuation is an important part of language mechanics. A good writer must be able to use punctuation properly. Consequently, this is a skill that will continue to be reinforced throughout your child's school career.

What Fourth Graders Should Know

In earlier grades most children simply write one long run-on sentence, but by fourth grade children are expected to know the finer points of punctuation and to correctly punctuate the end of a sentence with either periods, question marks, or exclamation marks. Fourth graders should be familiar with quotation marks, and they should also know how to use commas correctly to punctuate dates, items in a list, direct quotations, and dependent clauses. Fourth graders should understand how to correctly punctuate a letter, including the address, and how to use the apostrophe to make contractions and to show possession.

What You and Your Child Can Do

Write a Story. The more experience your child has with writing, the more comfortable she will be with correct punctuation. In this activity, encourage your child to write a story about a favorite hobby or experience. Let her use a computer if you have one since many children find this makes writing extra fun.

Take a Letter! Writing the addresses on envelopes is a good way to practice using capitalization rules. Don't miss an opportunity to let your child help you address holiday cards and invitations. Encourage her to write a letter to a hero, political leader, sports figure, musician, or athlete.

Have a Newspaper Search. This is a fun activity to do when your family is finished with the newspaper. Pick out an article appropriate for your child to read, and have her search for as many forms of punctuation as she can find.

Collect Postcards. Try to collect one postcard from each of the 50 states. Try writing letters to different schools or friends and family. In the letter writing process, you can use abbreviations for streets, states, and personal titles.

What Tests May Ask

As they do for grammar rules, most standardized tests today assess punctuation skills by testing a child's ability to *recognize* correct punctuation. On this type of test, a child must choose the correctly punctuated sentence, phrase, or term from four choices. Alternatively, a child might need to choose the correctly punctuated word or phrase in a given sentence from a group of incorrect choices.

Practice Skill: Punctuation

Directions: Choose the sentence that shows correct punctuation.

Example:

Ⓐ Billy, do you have a pen I could borrow.

Ⓑ I don't want to go to bed!

Ⓒ Susan come, here.

Ⓓ Jim went to collect something from the basement?

Answer:

Ⓑ I don't want to go to bed!

8 Ⓐ I need paper pens and ink.

Ⓑ If I'm going to make a cake, I'll need some flour eggs and, milk.

Ⓒ Do you want to bring a towel to the pool?

Ⓓ I am so tired I could, fall asleep right here.

9 Ⓐ After running home from school, the boys, ate some cookies.

Ⓑ She was born on August 15 1965.

Ⓒ When did you buy that coat?

Ⓓ The horse was the best jumper in the field?

Directions: Choose the correct abbreviation for the underlined word in the question.

10 My cousin Ariel lives at 123 Main <u>Street</u>.

Ⓐ st.

Ⓑ str.

Ⓒ St.

Ⓓ St

11 Ms. Danielle Jones
56 Music <u>Avenue</u>
Juniper, Alaska 56789

Ⓐ Av

Ⓑ ave.

Ⓒ Ave

Ⓓ Ave.

(See page 110 for the answer key.)

CHAPTER 7

Breaking It Down

Adults tend to take their ability to read for granted, forgetting the many years it took to master the high-level skills necessary for good reading comprehension. One way to make sure children understand what they read is to break down a story into various components, including the main idea, the setting, the characters, and the sequence of events.

A fourth grader's refined ability to read independently doesn't necessarily mean he will automatically grasp the main idea and be able to fully articulate the plot, or pay much attention to the setting and how the author uses description to enhance the story. That's why teachers spend a fair amount of time on these components, and why standardized testing will likely assess each area to see if a child is picking up these all-important clues. Knowing how well a child understands each component will provide a good picture of the child's overall reading comprehension.

Main Idea

Learning how to sum up the main idea of a piece of writing is really often quite difficult for most elementary students. While the ability to summarize a story is probably second nature to you, if you try to explain to your child how to go about it, you may begin to see why it can be so hard for them. While summarizing is probably something you have internalized and do automatically, it is not a skill children simply know.

They must learn how. You'd be surprised how many fourth graders are still trying to summarize by writing down every event that occurs in a story.

What Fourth Graders Should Know

By the end of fourth grade, most students have finally begun to understand how to sum up a story in a few sentences rather than simply retelling the entire passage. Many still need lots of practice, however, in not overlooking important points to include in a summary. Fourth graders also should be able to come up with alternate titles for stories that illustrate their grasp of the main idea.

What You and Your Child Can Do

Get Ready! Before starting to read a book together, spend some time talking about the main idea of the book with your child. What does he think it might be about just from looking at the cover illustration on the book?

Check Out Titles. One way to help your child learn to summarize is to focus on book titles, which ideally should sum up the entire story in a few words and predict what will be happening. The ability to provide a title for a story is important because it's closely related to the ability to understand the main idea.

Ask your child for an opinion about what a particular book might be about. Is *Little Women* a story about women? Then move on to the chapter titles. Ask your child if he can figure out what the chapter might be about by reading the titles. What other titles might he come up with?

Create Title Alternates. To boost your child's ability to summarize the main idea, brainstorm for "alternate titles" of story classics. Make them as funny as you want, but aim for a good summary of the story. Or choose a book without chapter titles, and have your child come up with his own.

Write Cover Blurbs. For a good example of what a summary should include, check out the back cover blurbs on your child's favorite books. How did the publisher decide to summarize the book? Look at books your child knows well so that he can see how a good summary is written. Remind your child that some back cover blurbs don't give complete summaries because the publisher is trying to entice the reader to read the book to find out more details.

Explore Textbooks. When working on learning how to summarize, don't ignore your child's textbooks. Social studies and history books are good choices for practice because most of these textbooks include helpful summary paragraphs either in the back or front of the chapters. (This is also a good way to enhance study skills!) Have your child read the chapter in his history book, and then show him the author's summary of the main points.

What Tests May Ask

Standardized tests for fourth graders will include some questions devoted to the main idea of a passage. Questions may ask a student to choose a sentence or phrase or title that best describes the main idea or topic of a passage.

Students also may be asked to identify the details in a passage that support the main idea. When answering questions about the main idea, students should read the title and the passage very carefully to help them decode the main idea.

Sequence

The ability to understand the sequence in a piece of writing requires the reader to figure out what comes first, next, and last in a story. It requires the ability to determine the main idea and supporting details, and how to retell stories. Both knowing how to summarize, and understanding the sequence of events are key skills in reading comprehension.

What Fourth Graders Should Know

In the fourth grade students are working with longer stories and looking for the clue words that help them figure out the order of the story. They are also dealing with stories that do not necessarily unfold in an immediately recognizable order.

What You and Your Child Can Do

Cooking. Take time to cook with your children; it will help enormously with the discipline of both following directions and understanding sequence of events. For even more benefit, have your child write down his own favorite recipe— and then make it! While your child probably knows how to make cinnamon sugar toast by heart, when he's forced to write down the steps, he may be surprised at the structure required to include all the steps in sequence.

Autobiography. Writing an autobiography is a wonderful way to help your child put the events of his own life into sequence. A fun way to help him keep these events straight is to have him make a time line for each year of his life. Have him note each important event that happened in each year (if you save your old calendars with all the activities written down, this should be a big help!). The first few years may be quite full, as so much happens in early childhood. Let your child check through his baby book for milestones. Have him type it up on the computer or write it out by hand, illustrate it, and create a colorful cover.

Five Generations. If your child likes to write, here's another fun project to help him learn sequencing. Instead of his own autobiography, have him write a history of five generations of his family. To help limit his job, ask your son to write a page for his father, grandfather, great-grandfather, and so on, for several generations. Have your daughter trace her mother, grand-mother, great-grandmother, and so on. This can give the family history more of a focus and help streamline the sequence of events.

Charting Books. During family reading time, review what has already been read in the story. Make sure you have the events in order. You might want to keep index cards or a chart with the information on it. (This is especially helpful if you're reading a biography of a person with many complicated family relationships, such as King Henry VIII, or a story with lots of characters.)

Comic Strip Scramble. Gather up your family's store of Sunday funnies and cut up your child's favorite comic strips. Mix them up, and have your child put them in correct sequence. What comes first? Next? Last?

What Tests May Ask

Standardized tests that assess sequencing ability may ask students to figure out how sentences are related to each other, or they may ask questions about the sequence of events in a passage—perhaps what the main character did and in what order. Tests may provide a variety of reading material to test students' sequencing skills, including stories, schedules, recipes, and time lines.

To do well on this type of test, students should remember to first read the passage to get an idea of what the story is about before answering questions. In questions focusing on sequence, they should be alert for signal words such as *first, later, after, then, finally,* and *at last.*

Practice Skill: Sequence

Directions: Read the passage and then answer the questions by choosing the correct answer.

Last week, Julie and Sue planned a day of holiday shopping. They decided to head out at 8:30 in the morning so that they would be first in line when the stores opened. First, they would go out to a restaurant for breakfast. After breakfast, they would drive to their favorite mall. They planned to visit the big department stores first. From there, they would go to some of the smaller shops to look for stocking stuffers. By then, it would be time for lunch. As they ate, they would check over their lists to see what they still needed to buy. At the last stop, they would pick up wrapping paper and ribbons. Finally, they would go home and rest their very tired feet.

Example:

What would Julie and Sue do while they ate their lunch?

(A) decide what stocking stuffers to buy

(B) plan what to eat for dinner

(C) pick out wrapping paper

(D) see what else they had to buy

Answer:

(D) see what else they had to buy

1 What is the last thing they would do?

(A) pick out wrapping paper

(B) buy cards

(C) rest their tired feet

(D) drive home

2 What is the first thing they would do?

(A) go to the mall

(B) write out lists

(C) go out to breakfast

(D) shop in the department stores

3 What is the last thing they would do before going to lunch?

(A) visit the smaller shops

(B) eat breakfast

(C) shop in the department stores

(D) go through their packages

Directions: Use the recipe below to answer the questions.

Cheesecake Cupcakes
From the kitchen of Dorothy "Grams" Malven

Ingredients:

3 eggs

½ cup sugar

1 pound of cream cheese

½ teaspoon vanilla

1 package vanilla wafers

1. Whip together eggs, sugar, and cheese until smooth.
2. Add vanilla.
3. Place 1 vanilla wafer in the bottom of cupcake liners.
4. Fill each liner half full with cheese mixture.
5. Bake at 350 degrees for 15 minutes.
6. Cool for 15 to 30 minutes or until the cupcakes fall.
7. Top with cherry, pineapple, or blueberry pie fillings.

Makes 2 dozen. These freeze well, but do not add topping before freezing.

Example:

What gets whipped together?

(A) cherry, pineapple, and blueberry pie filling

(B) eggs and a vanilla wafer

(C) eggs, sugar, and cheese

(D) eggs, sugar, cheese, and a vanilla wafer

Answer:

(C) eggs, sugar, and cheese

4 Which ingredient is **not** in the first step?

(A) eggs

(B) vanilla wafers

(C) sugar

(D) cheese

5 What should you **not** do before freezing the cupcakes?

(A) bake them

(B) mix the ingredients

(C) put the wafers in the cupcake liners

(D) put on the toppings

6 What is the second step?

(A) Bake.

(B) Mix the sugar, eggs, and cheese.

(C) Add vanilla.

(D) Put the vanilla wafers in the cupcake liners.

(See page 110 for the answer key.)

Characters and Settings

Characters and settings are the heart and soul of good literature, and a solid understanding of both is crucial in developing good reading comprehension skills. To understand a story, the reader needs to understand the characters, and taking note of the author's setting helps the reader understand what the author is trying to say.

What Fourth Graders Should Know

By fourth grade, you can expect your child to pay attention to a wide range of details in their favorite stories, including the setting and the range of characters. They should be able to understand the motivations of the main characters, in addition to the relationships among characters and how that may affect the story. Being able to understand and relate to the main characters can make the difference between a book that is read and forgotten and one that is destined to be wildly popular. The main reasons so many children respond to Harry Potter are his imperfections, the early injustice he's had to endure, and his plucky determination to persevere. Fourth graders are very good at understanding that well-drawn characters have both flaws and good points, and they may be able to articulate how these character traits affect the outcome of the plot.

What You and Your Child Can Do

Stage Set. Here's a good activity during story hour with your child—especially if the tale has a strong setting. After you finish reading the story, get out a big sheet of white paper and explore the structure you just read about. If your child just finished *Willy Wonka and the Chocolate Factory,* have him draw the factory with all its fanciful rooms full of candy and surprises, and wild characters.

Who's Who. After you finish reading a story with your child, or after your child finishes a book, have him draw a picture of his favorite character. Use the clues found in the book—what does the character look like? Wear?

Diorama. To ensure that your fourth grader is paying attention to the story's setting, have him make a diorama of a favorite scene. Most children love to make these special projects. Have him pay special attention to the clues the author gives about setting—housing, time of year, part of the world. Get a cardboard box and give your child paints, markers, fabric, glue, buttons, glitter—anything you can think of to make the diorama come alive.

What Tests May Ask

Standardized tests will probably assess your child's understanding of a character by presenting a passage and then asking him to answer questions about the character and the character's motivation. Your child should read the passage closely, looking for clues to figure out how the character feels and what the person is like. Likewise, questions about setting described in given passages can help determine if your child is paying attention to these important written clues.

Practice Skill: Characters and Settings

Directions: Read the passage. Choose the best answer to each question.

The Party

Ross dragged his feet as he walked behind his parents. They insisted that he come with them to this party for one of their neighbors. As one of the newest families on the block, his parents wanted to meet the other families and get to know their new neighbors.

But Ross was sure it would be a disaster. He didn't know anyone, and there were sure to be all grown-ups. Worse yet, his parents insisted he wear his Sunday suit. The collar itched and choked him as his parents rang the bell. Idly, he wondered whether doctors ever recorded a fatal illness caused by a collar that was too tight. As the door opened, he heard roars of laughter and loud party music. The room was filled with strangers.

How he missed his old neighborhood! On a day like this they would all be out in the ball field hitting grounders instead of going to a dopey party.

"Oh, good, you've brought your son!" he heard a woman say. "Come meet my boy!" Ross wanted to turn and run. What would the other boy think of him in this suit?

As he looked up, he saw another boy looking down at his shoes—and he was wearing a suit, too. The other boy looked up, saw Ross, and grinned. "Hey!" he whispered to Ross as his mother walked away. "You wanna go out back and hit some grounders?"

Example:

Why is Ross nervous?

Ⓐ He's worried about a test.

Ⓑ He is new in town.

Ⓒ He's performing in a play.

Ⓓ He forgot his baseball glove.

Answer:

Ⓑ He's new in town.

---

7 How does Ross feel?

Ⓐ excited about being in a new school

Ⓑ angry about leaving the old school

Ⓒ embarrassed about wearing a suit

Ⓓ happy to be going to a party

---

8 Where does this story take place?

Ⓐ in a school

Ⓑ in a classroom

Ⓒ at a park

Ⓓ in a neighbor's house

---

9 What is the location of this story like?

Ⓐ silent and empty

Ⓑ noisy and crowded

Ⓒ dark and scary

Ⓓ bright and hot

---

10 How does Ross probably feel when the other boy grins at him?

Ⓐ angry

Ⓑ relieved

Ⓒ lonesome

Ⓓ mad

(See page 110 for the answer key.)

CHAPTER 8

Reading Comprehension

Reading comprehension—that is, understanding what has been read—is of great importance in fourth grade, as students become more adept at understanding stories in general. No longer do children this age have to struggle along, pausing to puzzle out every few words they encounter. Reading comprehension is considered to be a high-order skill that involves putting together a whole series of concepts, including summarizing, making predictions, sequencing, and drawing conclusions.

Reading Critically

What Fourth Graders Should Know

Fourth graders have entered the ranks of critical readers—they are much more comfortable in reading and understanding on many levels than they were even a year ago. Most fourth graders can understand cause and effect relationships, predict outcomes, and draw conclusions based on the information they have read. They can pick out the implied feelings and motivations of characters, which allows them to compare and contrast one story or idea with another.

What You and Your Child Can Do

Reading. It's not too late to start if you've been neglecting reading to your child, and you should continue if you have been reading out loud for some time. Reading out loud helps your child get used to following the thread of a story and understanding the events as she hears them.

Continue reading to her and let her read to you.

Magazines. Subscribe to age-appropriate magazines such as *Stone Soup, American Girl,* or *National Geographic Junior.*

Just the Facts, Ma'am. Encourage your child to read a variety of newspapers, and give her the "who what where when and why" quiz. Point out short articles in a newspaper or magazine that you think would interest her. After she's finished reading, ask her the "who what where when and why" of the article, and see how many she can get right.

Other Eyes. This activity is a good way to get your child to think about how the story might change if it were told from another perspective. This activity works very well for tales with a strong moral. For example, if you're reading a story about a girl and her horse, ask your child to think about how the story would be different if told from the horse's perspective.

Helping Your Child. You can boost your child's comprehension by encouraging her to make predictions as she reads; compare and contrast stories, characters, and settings; and talk about causes and effects.

Jumping Ahead. Sometimes when parents read a really exciting book to a child at night, they find that during the next day the child reads ahead to find out what happens. If this occurs in your house, don't scold! Just ask her to summarize the chapters you've missed, and keep going.

Cause and Effect

Children learn at an early age that actions have consequences. They learn that touching a hot stove causes a burn, or that smacking a sibling could lead to trouble. As children get older, they begin to understand that many actions have a variety of effects. They learn that putting water in the freezer creates ice, and that if they do something kind for friends, their friends will do something nice in return.

The cause is *why* something happens, and the effect is *what* happens. It takes practice and sometimes a bit of persistence for children to work comfortably in the realm of cause and effect, but eventually the concept does click.

What Fourth Graders Should Know

Fourth graders know very well that for every cause, there is an effect. If they don't clean their plate, they can't have dessert. If they don't rake the leaves when Dad asks them to, they will get in trouble. They have learned that stories can be relied upon to have causes and effects too. Something happens in a story and something else occurs as a result.

What You and Your Child Can Do

Family Reading. During your family reading time, discuss what happens to the characters and why. If the main character gets grounded for the weekend, discuss why it happened. Make sure to explain that being grounded is the effect and that not feeding the dog is the cause.

Science at Home. Home-based fun science experiments are a good way to learn cause and effect. Ask your child to try to predict what will happen, and then see if the predictions come true.

Before That! Take every chance you can to point out cause and effect by asking your child to imagine what happened just before. If you see a car stopped by the edge of the road with its fender dented and another car next to it, ask your child to imagine what happened right before this.

What Tests May Ask

Standardized tests for the fourth grade usually assess cause and effect by presenting a passage and then asking questions based on the information contained in the passage. To answer the questions, students must understand what happened in the story and be able to infer what caused something to happen. Students should look for word clues such as *because, so, since,* or *as a result* that indicate cause and effect.

Practice Skill: Cause and Effect

Directions: Identify as cause or effect the underlined words in each question.

Example:

> Jane grabbed a book from her sister, and she was punished by her mother.

(A) cause

(B) effect

(C) neither

(D) both

Answer:

(A) cause

---

1 Andrea went to the doctor's because she had a sore throat and a fever.

(A) cause

(B) effect

(C) neither

(D) both

---

2 Jason's lizard got loose, so <u>he was late for school</u>.

   Ⓐ cause   Ⓑ effect

   Ⓒ neither   Ⓓ both

3 <u>Samantha joined ballet</u> after her best friend Rachael did.

   Ⓐ cause   Ⓑ effect

   Ⓒ neither   Ⓓ both

4 <u>Erin and Laura threw a party</u> for Cassandra's sixteenth birthday.

   Ⓐ cause   Ⓑ effect

   Ⓒ neither   Ⓓ both

(See page 110 for the answer key.)

Compare and Contrast

Students learn about comparing and contrasting in earlier grades, but in fourth grade they are expected to improve this skill. To find similarities and differences, they need to be able to look past the obvious and look for the unseen. For instance, if they are comparing two classmates, Katie and Justin, they may draw up a table like this:

KATIE	KATIE AND JUSTIN	JUSTIN
girl	fourth graders	boy
brown hair	same birthday	blonde hair
likes horses	play soccer	allergic to animals
has one brother/ one sister		has one sister
middle child		oldest child

The idea is to encourage children to look beyond the obvious—he's a boy and she's a girl. This involves using metaphors and similes and recognizing what is being compared.

What You and Your Child Can Do

Be a Comparison Shopper. Help your child become a comparison shopper. Instead of handing over money for birthdays or holidays, try giving your child one of the new store "gift cards" that look like credit cards but are really just gift certificates with a set amount. Most children love to shop with a "credit card" just like Mom or Dad. You'll be amazed at how carefully a child with one of these cards will investigate every toy in the store to get the best value for her money. If she doesn't seem to know where to start with her comparisons, help her: "This toy is very well made, but that one looks as though it would break after two uses. This toy has good play value, but that one looks like something you'd get tired of very quickly."

Family Reading. Pick two different characters in the book the family is reading, and compare them. Choose one your child liked and one she didn't. Ask her why she did or didn't like the characters.

Movie Reviews. Watch a movie together, and then read the newspaper reviews. Compare how different critics rated the movie, and then discuss your feelings with your child. How did your child's impressions compare to the critics'?

What Tests May Ask

On typical standardized tests for fourth grade, students may be asked to identify what two things are being compared, or what something or someone is being compared to.

Practice Skill: Compare and Contrast

Directions: Choose which two people, places, or things are being compared in each question.

Example:

Atlantic City is almost as exciting and fun as Las Vegas.

- (A) fun and Atlantic City
- (B) exciting and Las Vegas
- (C) fun and Las Vegas
- (D) Atlantic City and Las Vegas

Answer:

- (D) Atlantic City and Las Vegas

---

5 Grandpa's pancakes are not as fluffy and tasty as Grandma's.

- (A) Grandpa and Grandma
- (B) Grandpa's pancakes and Grandma's pancakes
- (C) tasty and fluffy
- (D) pancakes and waffles

---

6 Theresa and Marcia have the same birthday, March 17.

- (A) Theresa and Marcia
- (B) birthday and March 17
- (C) Theresa and birthday
- (D) Marcia and birthday

---

7 The herd of sheep moved across the road slower than molasses.

- (A) sheep and road
- (B) sheep and herd
- (C) sheep and molasses
- (D) moved and slower

8 Andrew ran a faster race than Mel at the state championships.

- (A) Mel and race
- (B) Andrew and race
- (C) district championships and state championships
- (D) Mel and Andrew

(See page 110 for the answer key.)

Predicting Outcomes

Being able to predict the outcome of a story will help improve a child's reading comprehension. To be a good reader, she will have to become a good guesser: What might the character do next? What might happen in the next paragraph? How might the story end?

What Fourth Graders Should Know

Fourth graders should be very good at predicting outcomes by picking out clues from the story, title, and illustrations. By this age, most fourth graders are such confident risk takers that they are ready to make some intelligent guesses about how the story will turn out.

What You and Your Child Can Do

Sherlock Holmes. Just like the great detective, your child should form a habit of predicting events by what she observes. Ask her to predict everyday things in her life—not just the outcomes of stories. When you go out to eat, ask her to predict what Sis is going to order. What will she get for her birthday? While waiting in the airport, ask her to predict what the woman across the room does for a living. Are there any clues in her clothes or attitude?

Practicing. You can help your child learn to take risks by making lots of predictions. When you choose a story together, ask: Why might you like this story? As you begin to read, ask her what she thinks the story is about. What does she think might happen next?

Magazine Roulette. When you're in a bookstore, stop by the magazine section with your child. Look at the story and article titles in the magazines, and ask her to predict what she thinks the stories and articles might be about. Choose magazines that are designed to be of interest to children.

What Tests May Ask

Standardized tests for fourth grade will assess students' ability to predict outcomes by presenting a passage and asking children to predict what will happen next and what might happen in the end. Tests also may present a title and ask students to predict what the story or article might be about.

Practice Skill: Predicting Outcomes

Directions: Read the passage. Choose the best answer for each question.

The U.S. Treasury once printed a $100,000 bill. It was illustrated with the head of Salmon Portland Chase, the Secretary of the Treasury during the Civil War. None of these bills have been printed since 1955. Only 348 of these bills remain in circulation.

Example:

What is the best title for this passage?

Ⓐ The Largest Unit of Money Ever Made

Ⓑ The Life and Times of Salmon Chase

Ⓒ Your Money

Ⓓ It Happened During the Civil War

Answer:

Ⓐ The Largest Unit of Money Ever Made

Story

A piano is a keyboard instrument. When the pianist touches the black and white keys, the keys hit small hammers. The hammers strike the strings that stretch from one end of the piano to the other. The strings make different sounds according to their length.

9 What is the best title for this passage?

Ⓐ How to Play Music

Ⓑ Ludwig von Beethoven: His Life

Ⓒ How a Piano Works

Ⓓ I Like to Play Music

10 What is a book titled *It Came from the Murky Depths* most likely about?

Ⓐ a funny story about a goose and a rooster

Ⓑ a mystery involving secrets in an old mansion

Ⓒ a cozy story about a family of fishermen

Ⓓ a scary story about a monster from the depths of a loch

11 Which would be the best title for a book about Santa Claus's life?

Ⓐ The Life and Adventures of Santa Claus

Ⓑ Lots of Toys

Ⓒ Holiday Memories

Ⓓ Shopping Is Fun

Directions: Read the following passage and then choose the sentence that describes what would logically happen next.

Sylvia pulled up the sheet and smoothed out the wrinkles. Next, she pulled up the blankets and turned the sheet over the top. She fluffed the pillows and place them carefully on top of the bed.

12 (A) Finally, she fluffed the quilt and smoothed it over the top of the bed.

     (B) She threw the ball for her dog.

     (C) She curled up under the blankets and went to sleep.

     (D) Finally, she raised her hand to answer a question.

Directions: Read the following passage. Choose the statement that best describes what the story will probably be about.

Insects are animals that don't have bones inside their bodies like people do. Instead, they have a hard covering outside.

13 (A) The story will probably be a scary mystery.

     (B) The story will probably be very funny.

     (C) The story will probably be a sad story about a poor family.

     (D) The story will probably be about science facts.

(See page 110 for the answer key.)

Drawing Conclusions

A *conclusion* is a kind of decision that a person makes as a result of certain clues. If you walk into your child's classroom and see balloons everywhere and everyone eating ice cream as one child blows out candles on a cake, you can conclude that someone is having a birthday. In reading, your child will be expected to gather the clues planted by the author and come to her own conclusions based on those clues.

What Fourth Graders Should Know

By fourth grade the ability to perceive the deeper meanings embedded in many stories continues to grow. Children this age may surprise you with their sensitive ability to perceive motivations and reach conclusions. This means your child has developed not only the ability to understand the words presented but also to draw inferences from sometimes-subtle wording and implied action.

What You and Your Child Can Do

Ask Questions. You can help your child learn how to reach conclusions and make inferences by gently guiding her to gather clues and sum up what she's learned so far about a particular story. For example, let's say your child reads a book about an immigrant mother and father who go through terrible trials in order to provide a better life for their new baby. You can ask your child what conclusions she can make about this mother and father. You're looking for an answer along these lines: They are loving parents who take good care of their children and who are willing to make sacrifices for their children.

Read between the Lines. As you finish a story with your child, ask questions that require her to have read between the lines in reaching conclusions about the story. The author may not come right out and describe everything exactly, but your child should still be able to reach some conclusions based on subtle clues the author provides.

What Tests May Ask

Standardized tests will assess how well your child can make conclusions and draw inferences from written material by presenting a story and asking questions about it. Your child should read the entire passage first, looking for clues to help answer the questions. Once she draws a conclusion about what she's read, she should look for at least two details in the passage to support her answer.

Practice Skill: Drawing Conclusions

Directions: Read the following passage, and choose the correct answer for each question.

Jim and David were walking home from school, their boots wet with mud and their rain slickers buttoned up under their chins. They came across a crowd of children in the schoolyard. It was a fight, and one boy was lying on the ground in the mud. As Jim and David ran over, the crowd suddenly fled. Jim bent down to help the struggling boy on the ground. Suddenly, a hand closed over his collar. "Stop fighting!" the principal bellowed.

Example:

You can tell from the story that the weather is

Ⓐ rainy.   Ⓑ hot and humid.

Ⓒ icy cold.   Ⓓ snowing.

Answer:

Ⓐ rainy.

14 What will probably happen next?

Ⓐ The boys will happily run off for ice cream cones.

Ⓑ The principal will expect to punish Jim for fighting.

Ⓒ Jim will fall asleep.

Ⓓ The boys will take a math test.

15 Who is Jim?

Ⓐ David's uncle

Ⓑ David's father

Ⓒ David's friend

Ⓓ a stranger

16 Why did the crowd run away when Jim and David approached?

Ⓐ They were tired of watching the fight.

Ⓑ They saw the principal approaching.

Ⓒ They were hungry.

Ⓓ It was time to go home.

(See page 110 for the answer key.)

CHAPTER 9

Literary Genres

A student's ability to read and interpret information from many different types of literature is crucial. In fourth grade children are expected to gather information from a variety of contexts such as biography, poetry, fiction, and nonfiction. Children of this age should be able to identify a major idea or theme in a piece of writing, and most can write comfortably in a variety of forms, including poetry, fantasy, fiction, and nonfiction.

The goal of fourth grade is to increase competency, interest, and level of comprehension in reading using a variety of reading materials, including novels, poems, nonfiction periodicals and books, plays, and myths.

Facts versus Opinions

To be an informed reader, it's important to be able to sift through what is indisputable fact from what a person supposes to be true. A *fact* is simply a piece of information—Harrisburg is the capital of Pennsylvania. An opinion is a statement about what someone thinks or believes—Harrisburg is a beautiful city.

What Fourth Graders Should Know

By fourth grade, children understand the difference between fact and opinion, and they can discuss and give examples of all genres of literature and can reproduce them in their own writing.

Fourth graders spend a fair amount of time learning to sift through facts versus opinion. The key to doing well with this task is to know some of the clue words that indicate an opinion.

You can help your child recognize these words that herald an opinion:

my opinion

I think

might be

an idea

it looks like

it seems

What You and Your Child Can Do

Magazine Articles. Get your child a subscription to a magazine such as *American Girl, Boy's Life, Time for Kids,* or *National Geographic's World.* Read through the articles with him. As you read, see if you can identify facts and opinions. Help him to understand that some of the statements are factual and some are the author's opinion.

Letters to the Editor. Read some of the letters to the editor in your local paper to find examples of both facts and opinions. Your child may want to write a letter of his own to the editor.

Fun Ads. Have your child write and illustrate an advertisement for a fictional product. Let him be as outrageous as he wants. Discuss how an advertisement may contain opinion, not just the facts. Or have him "produce" an ad for the "radio"—let him record it on tape, complete with sound effects. If you're feeling really creative, help him create a script for a "TV" ad for a product, and help him film it with a video camera.

The Film Critic. If there's anyone who's opinionated, it's a film critic. Let your child act as your family "movie critic." Let him rent a video, and then create a brief opinion essay about why he liked it—or didn't like it. Have him describe the show (the facts) and then give a rating (his opinion). Point out the difference.

The Book Reviewer. If he's more a reader than a TV fan, let him "review" his favorite book. Again, get him to provide a brief summary (facts) followed by his opinion of the book (opinion). Many children's magazines accept book reviews; help him investigate a possible outlet to publish his review.

What Tests May Ask

Standardized tests will probably assess whether your child can tell the difference between fact and opinion by presenting a passage and then asking questions about whether each idea in the passage is a fact or opinion. To decide which is which, your child should look for something that can be proven true, something that's a fact. Feelings or beliefs are opinions. He should also be on the alert for the opinion word clues listed earlier.

Practice Skill: Facts versus Opinions

Directions: Choose the correct statement to answer each question.

Example:

Which statement is a fact?

Ⓐ Niharika and her brother are from India.

Ⓑ I think that's the largest pumpkin in the world!

Ⓒ That is the most beautiful cactus in the shop.

Ⓓ Abraham Lincoln was a wonderful president.

Answer:

Ⓐ Niharika and her brother are from India.

1 Which statement is an opinion?

Ⓐ Gabriella was born on September 14, 1996.

Ⓑ Her parents are Jennifer and Paul.

Ⓒ She is the cutest little girl.

Ⓓ She lives in New York.

2 Which statement is **not** a fact?

Ⓐ Cows have four feet.

Ⓑ The sun is a star.

Ⓒ Cats are the best pets.

Ⓓ A German shepherd is a dog.

3 Which statement is **not** an opinion?

Ⓐ Dogs are good pets.

Ⓑ Stacy is my younger sister.

Ⓒ Mysteries are the best books to read on vacation.

Ⓓ Quilting is easy to do.

4 Which statement is an opinion?

Ⓐ Vegetables are good for you.

Ⓑ Candy corn is not a vegetable.

Ⓒ Pumpkins are a squash.

Ⓓ The best vegetable is cauliflower.

NEWS SCOOP FROM MISS CALLAHAN'S ROOM

November 15, 2002   Volume 1 Issue 2

Students Walk to Raise Money for Homeless Shelter

Students at Eastern Elementary School this week raised more than $200 for a local shelter. Each student contributed a few dollars and then walked to a neighboring church. The walk for grades 2 through 8 was approximately 2 miles long. Students in kindergarten and first grade had a shorter walk to Jones Park and back. Students, teachers, and a few parents all walked together.

The students responded positively to the experience. Teddy in grade one said, "It was fun." Allison in kindergarten said, "I liked going to the park." Jaina, grade two, responded happily, "It was a long walk, but I had fun waving to the cars." Third grader Eric thought it "was cool to walk with everyone." Alex, a fourth grader, said, "I had fun, but I was tired when I got done." Jessica, an eighth grader, commented, "I think it was important for us to do something nice for someone else."

The walk was a success for everyone.

Directions: Use the story above to answer the following questions.

Example:

Which of the following statements is **not** a fact from the story?

(A) The students in grades 2 through 8 walked 2 miles.

(B) The kindergartners and first graders walked to Jones Park and back.

(C) The money raised went to a local shelter.

(D) Only teachers and students went on the walk.

Answer:

(D) Only teachers and students went on the walk.

---

5 Which of these opinions was **not** expressed in the story?

(A) It was boring.

(B) It was fun.

(C) It was cool.

(D) It was long.

---

6 Which of these statements is a fact about the walk described in the story?

(A) The school walks every year.

(B) Only Miss Callahan's class goes on the walk.

(C) The students did not have fun on the walk.

(D) The school raised more than $200 for the shelter.

(See page 110 for the answer key.)

Character Analysis

What Fourth Graders Should Know

Students in the fourth grade have made a transition in reading and are now expected to use and evaluate the information they are given. They are asked to make judgments about characters based on the information they read; sometimes the answers are given and other times they must be inferred. They must learn to think about the traits and values of the characters in their books so that they will know how a person's actions and words can reveal crucial information.

What You and Your Child Can Do

Family Reading. Spend time reading as a family. Discuss the characters. What do you know about the characters? How do you know this? Look for specific examples to support your impressions.

Autobiographies. This activity has been mentioned before in other contexts, but it can also be a good way for your child to learn how to analyze characters in stories and people in real life. Have your child discover things about himself. If he decides he is an "animal person," he needs to come up with evidence. Perhaps he volunteers at the local animal shelter. Maybe he has three cats, two dogs, and an iguana. These facts would be strong evidence to support his contention that he is "an animal person."

What Tests May Ask

In assessing a fourth grader's skill at character analysis, standardized tests may present a passage about one or several characters and then ask students to answer questions pertaining to the characters.

Practice Skill: Character Analysis

Directions: Read the passage and then answer the questions.

Meaghan was tired when she got home from her long day at school and her volunteer work. Today was Friday, her favorite day of the week—even though it was also her longest. Right after school she went to the animal shelter, where she was a "petter." She would spend 10 minutes playing with and petting each of the animals, making sure each one got some individual attention.

Example:

Meaghan is a _____ girl.

(A) boring   (B) busy

(C) lazy   (D) mean

Answer:

(B) busy

7   How does Meaghan feel about animals?

(A) She is allergic to them.

(B) She does not care for them.

(C) She is indifferent about them.

(D) She cares for them a lot.

Tony ran into the house out of breath with a big grin. He couldn't wait to share his big news with his family. He could not believe the luck he had at the game. It had started out as just another soccer game, but then it all changed in the second half when the coach gave him the chance of a lifetime. All he could think about on the way home was how to tell his family the news. But where were they? Why wasn't his family home?

8   What was Tony's mood when he came home from the soccer game?

(A) disappointed   (B) angry

(C) excited   (D) depressed

9   How did you know how Tony felt?

(A) He had a grin on his face.

(B) The whole soccer game was bad.

(C) He said he had a bad day at school.

(D) The coach did not let him play in the game.

10   If his family is not home, how will he feel?

(A) happy   (B) disappointed

(C) excited   (D) joyful

Miss Callahan went to her classroom to find her attendance slip for the office. She couldn't believe she had forgotten it. She remembered writing it out; she was sure she had given it to the messenger. If she didn't send it to the office, what happened to it? She searched through the papers on her desk. It had to be there. Or had her desk eaten that paper too?

11 Which word best describes Miss Callahan?

Ⓐ organized

Ⓑ tidy

Ⓒ disorganized

Ⓓ neat

12 How does Miss Callahan feel at this moment in the story?

Ⓐ happy

Ⓑ sad

Ⓒ frustrated

Ⓓ excited

(See page 110 for the answer key.)

Reality versus Fantasy

The difference between what is real and what is only imagined is an important one in literature. By fourth grade students should be able to tell the difference between reality and fantasy stories, and they should be ready to read more complex examples of fantasy.

What Fourth Graders Should Know

In fourth grade, in-depth study of fantasy continues, and students read a wide range of classic fantasy stories. They are taught to compare these forms of literature with reality-based stories. At this age, the fantasy series of *Harry Potter,* the *Chronicles of Narnia,* and the *Unicorn Chronicles* are all favorites.

What You and Your Child Can Do

Reality Check. As you read a child's fantasy book (such as Madeleine L'Engle's *A Wind in the Door*), discuss with your child the difference between reality and fantasy. Using a notebook, set up a chart on a fresh sheet of paper. On one side of the page, write "reality," and on the other, "fantasy." After reading a chapter in *Wind,* take turns writing sentences about incidents in the book, putting those that could really happen under "reality" and those that couldn't happen under "fantasy":

REALITY	FANTASY
Meg is worried about her brother.	There is such a thing as a cherubim.
Charles Wallace makes hot cocoa.	Meg travels into Charles' mitochondrion.

What Tests May Ask

Standardized tests in fourth grade usually assess a child's understanding of the difference between reality and fantasy by presenting a passage and asking the child to discern which statements are true and which are fantasy.

Practice Skill: Reality versus Fantasy

Directions: Choose the correct answers for the following questions.

Example:

Which of these sentences is true?

Ⓐ Jupiter has two moons.

Ⓑ Humans can breathe underwater with their gills.

Ⓒ Cats can sing.

Ⓓ There are such things as whangdoodles.

Answer:

Ⓐ Jupiter has two moons.

---

13 Which of these sentences is based on fantasy?

Ⓐ Brooms can fly.

Ⓑ Microwaves can boil water in seconds.

Ⓒ Spaceships can fly to the moon.

Ⓓ Submarines can dive underwater.

---

14 Which of these sentences is based on fantasy?

Ⓐ Dragons do exist.

Ⓑ An artificial heart can help a person live.

Ⓒ An air tank can help a diver breathe underwater.

Ⓓ Braces will straighten your teeth.

(See page 110 for the answer key.)

Biography

Biographies are an important part of most fourth-grade classrooms. This genre combines literature with history or current events, as students learn about the lives of important people in sports, science, medicine, government, and history. No matter what interests your child may have, it should be possible to find a biography that he'll enjoy reading.

What Fourth Graders Should Know

Fourth graders should be quite familiar with the kind of information they will find in a biography, and they should have read at least one example in class. Many classrooms keep special sections or libraries exclusively devoted to a wide variety of biographies.

What You and Your Child Can Do

Family Bio. If you really want your child to understand what goes into a biography, help him write a biography of a family member. Armed with a tape recorder (or video camera), let him interview family members. Then let him choose one family member to write a biography about. Gather photos of that person, and have him illustrate the photos with a story of that person's life. Fourth graders who are confident with technology (either video cameras, digital cameras, or even a simple point – n – shoot) can record the biography in any media they wish. The objectives of this project are to make sure that they capture the elements of a good biography—and that they know how to record the important points of a person's life.

The Tonight Show. After your child reads a biography, ask him to pretend he is the character, and ask him all kinds of questions: "So, Mr. President, how did you feel on the day you were elected?"

Write His Life Story. Some children may do better writing their own life stories than writing those of others. And why not let him? After all, the odds are that he knows his own life better than he knows anyone else's. Make sure he includes all of the most important events that have occurred so far. (Making a brief outline of his life might help him organize his thoughts.)

Book Bio. After your child finishes reading a favorite book, have him write a biography of one of the characters in the book. For example, if he loves *Harry Potter,* have him write a biography about a minor character in the series—perhaps one of the lesser-known Hogwarts' teachers.

What Tests May Ask

Most standardized tests present a brief biographical sketch and then ask children a series of questions about the passage. These questions may ask children to determine the genre of the passage, or they may ask specific questions about one aspect of the passage.

Practice Skill: Biography

Directions: Read the following passage. Choose the correct answer to each question.

J. K. (Joanne Kathleen) Rowling grew up in Chipping, a small town in England. She always wanted to be a writer and wrote her first "book" at the age of six—a story about a rabbit called Rabbit. She graduated from Exeter University and then worked in London and France. She got the idea for the Harry Potter series on a long train ride. She wrote in cafés and pubs during lunch; by the time her daughter was born, her book was one-quarter finished. She now lives in Edinburgh and still writes in cafés.

Example:

J. K. Rowling was

Ⓐ the first writer in space.

Ⓑ the creator of Mickey Mouse.

Ⓒ the author of the *Harry Potter* series.

Ⓓ a major TV star.

Answer:

Ⓒ the author of the *Harry Potter* series.

---

15 Rowling was raised

Ⓐ in France.

Ⓑ in Portugal.

Ⓒ near a train station.

Ⓓ in England.

---

16 Rowling got the idea for her book series

Ⓐ in a café.

Ⓑ in a restaurant.

Ⓒ on a train.

Ⓓ on a plane.

---

17 Rowling's first book was about

Ⓐ wizards and witches.

Ⓑ dogs and cats.

Ⓒ a rabbit.

Ⓓ a bear.

Mohandas Gandhi was a founder of the free nation of India. For many years he fought to free his country from Great Britain's rule. However, unlike many people who have fought for freedom in the past, Gandhi did not believe in war or violence. He earned the name "Mahatma," which means "Great Soul," because of his reverence for peace.

18 Gandhi is remembered as

Ⓐ a ruler of Great Britain.

Ⓑ a great man of peace who fought for freedom for India.

Ⓒ a leader of the American civil rights movement.

Ⓓ a scientist and inventor.

---

19 He was called "Mahatma" because

Ⓐ he had many wives.

Ⓑ he was a king of India.

Ⓒ his people thought he was a "great soul."

Ⓓ he was a rich man.

(See page 110 for the answer key.)

Poetry

What Fourth Graders Should Know

The study of poetry in fourth grade continues, showing students how poets use rhythm and words to create images. Because a poem can be short—and doesn't always have to conform to traditional rules—poetry appeals even to reluctant readers. Good poetry books for this age include *For Laughing Out Loud, Poems to Tickle Your Funnybone,* by Jack Prelutsky and *Where the Sidewalk Ends* by Shel Silverstein.

What You and Your Child Can Do

Read Aloud. Have your child read his favorite poems out loud to you—poetry usually sounds best when read aloud. Ask your child what he likes about the poems, what the poems make him feel. Discuss the poems further, asking specific questions about the poets' intentions. You want to help your child boost his comprehension of poetry.

Write Poetry. Encourage your child to try writing some poems, and remind him that they don't have to rhyme. Stimulate his interest by getting him to write a list of nouns, and then a list of adjectives, and then a list of verbs on slips of paper. Mix them up, draw one of each, and try to combine them into a phrase or poem. This activity can jump-start creativity and get your child thinking of poems in new, unusual ways.

Enter a Poetry Contest. Urge your child to enter poetry contests for fun and prizes. Have him check out literary magazines such as *Stone Soup* or online poetry Web sites that offer contests. Try *The Number 1 Poetry Site for Kids on the Web:* www.gigglepoetry.com/contests.html.

What Tests May Ask

Standardized tests will probably test students' understanding of poetry by presenting a poem or part of a poem and then asking specific questions about the poet's intentions, specific themes, and so on.

Practice Skill: Poetry

Directions: Read the poem. Then answer the following questions about the poem.

The Wind
By Robert Louis Stevenson

I saw you toss the kites on high
And blow the birds about the sky;
And all around I heard you pass,
Like ladies' skirts across the grass—
    O wind, a-blowing all day long,
    O wind, that sings so loud a song!

I saw the different things you did,
But always you yourself you hid.
I felt you push, I heard you call,
I could not see yourself at all—
    O wind, a-blowing all day long,
    O wind, that sings so loud a song!

O you that are so strong and cold,
O blower, are you young or old?
Are you a beast of field and tree,
Or just a stronger child than me?
    O wind, a-blowing all day long,
    O wind, that sings so loud a song!

Example:

What is this poem about?

Ⓐ   a bully on the playground

Ⓑ   a major storm

Ⓒ   the wind

Ⓓ   a blizzard

Answer:

Ⓒ   the wind

20   What does the poet compare the wind to?

Ⓐ   kites

Ⓑ   ladies' skirts

Ⓒ   birds

Ⓓ   kittens

21 What does the poet mean when he says "I saw the different things you did, But always you yourself you hid"?

(A) The subject of the poem is destructive.

(B) The subject of the poem is a thief.

(C) The subject of the poem is shy.

(D) The subject of the poem is invisible.

(See page 110 for the answer key.)

CHAPTER 10

Study Skills

The importance of study skills (also called *learning strategies*) can't be overstated. Solid strategies for conducting research and understanding reference material will be necessary for your child for at least the next 8 to 12 years of education.

Because these skills are so important, you can expect standardized tests to assess how well your child has mastered them. Fourth graders normally are expected to be able to alphabetize words, find information in a dictionary, read graphs and charts, and recognize and know how to use the various parts of a book.

School changes quite dramatically for students in fourth grade. Your child will be applying reading skills in a variety of subjects, and study skills will become very important as students this year will be asked to write reports and handle long-term assignments.

Your child will be expected to alphabetize easily to the third letter, look up words by using guide words on a reference book page, and understand dictionary entries. Students will also continue to use reference material and explore the parts of a reference book.

Alphabetical Order

Students in the fourth grade have been working with alphabetical order for at least two years at this point. Teachers encourage this ability to develop in children because it is an important foundation to mastering study skills and using reference materials. Students need to under-stand alphabetical ordering to effectively use a dictionary, encyclopedia, and thesaurus, among many other reference materials.

What Fourth Graders Should Know

Children this age should be able to alphabetize at least to the third, and possibly the fourth letter. However, there are a few areas that make alphabetical order a challenge for many fourth graders. Many children are simply overwhelmed by the number of words they must sort through and by putting words in order to the third or fourth letter in the word. A trick to help get students through this mental block is to have them cross out the letters as they compare the words. When they come to the letter that is different, they can underline it and decide which one comes first in order.

What You and Your Child Can Do

Keep an Address Book. Have your child keep an address book for friends and family. You can either buy her a special address book or have her create her own. Whatever the method, you can begin by having her sort friends' names alphabetically before entering them in the book.

Assign Postal Duty. When the family mail comes in each day, have your child sort it and then put it in alphabetical order. Because there aren't so many items, this easy task will provide your child with certain success and practice.

Write Grocery Lists. In an effort to help make your shopping easier—and to provide practice—ask your child to put the weekly grocery list in alphabetical order.

Practice! There are so many opportunities for alphabetization around the house. If your child likes to cook, put her to work alphabetizing your spices. If she loves to read, assign her one book-shelf and ask her to put the shelf in alphabeti-cal order by author. If she has a big collection of Beanie Babies, have her line them up by name in alphabetical order.

What Tests May Ask

Standardized tests assess alphabetical order primarily in the context of using dictionaries and encyclopedias. Students will usually be expected to be able to alphabetize to the third (and sometimes the fourth) letter.

Practice Skill: Alphabetical Order

Directions: Choose the word that would be first in alphabetical order.

Example:

- (A) leaf
- (B) tree
- (C) flower
- (D) seed

Answer:

- (C) flower

1 (A) sofa
   (B) pillow
   (C) pumpkin
   (D) television

2 (A) spoon
   (B) spatula
   (C) trivet
   (D) stove

3 (A) John
   (B) Josephine
   (C) Jessica
   (D) Jamie

4 (A) bath
   (B) batter
   (C) batten
   (D) battle

Directions: Choose the group of words that is in correct alphabetical order. If none of the groups are correct choose **not here.**

Example:

- (A) paper, pen, pencil
- (B) marker, crayon, pen
- (C) scissors, exacto-knife, cutter
- (D) not here

Answer:

- (A) paper, pen, pencil

5 (A) compact disk, record, tape
   (B) rock, classical, jazz
   (C) stereo, radio, walkman
   (D) not here

6 Ⓐ cats, chinchillas, chimpanzees

   Ⓑ dogs, hedgehogs, lizards

   Ⓒ monkeys, zebras, bears

   Ⓓ not here

7 Ⓐ tulips, roses, pansies

   Ⓑ pumpkins, gourds, squash

   Ⓒ asparagus, broccoli, corn

   Ⓓ not here

8 Ⓐ run, stretch, tug

   Ⓑ hop, skip, jump

   Ⓒ captain, alligator, tree

   Ⓓ not here

(See page 110 for the answer key.)

Dictionaries

Being able to "use a dictionary" involves the ability to find the meanings, spellings, and pronunciations of the words. It also includes the abilities to use guide words located at the tops of the pages and to understand the derivations of words. Students need to know the parts of a dictionary and what they are used for in order to make good use of this valuable reference tool.

What Fourth Graders Should Know

Fourth graders have been using the dictionary for at least a year, but many are still struggling to find specific words when directed to do so. Fourth graders may still need help in finding and using guide words. Many times they open to a page with the correct first letter of the word and then become frustrated because they can't find the word they're looking for.

Fourth graders also may be confused about looking up a word using its base word, and they may get confused in finding words with suffixes such as *-s, -ed, -ing,* and *-ly.*

What You and Your Child Can Do

Assign a Word of the Day (or Week). Have your family learn a new word on a regular basis as mentioned in previous chapters. Look up a new word in the dictionary. Discuss the new word at the dinner table, and check out all of the information you can find about it in the dictionary. If the origin of the word is given, read that too. Find out how it is spelled by itself and with endings. Look at how different endings change the base word into different parts of speech. Be brave—pick words that make use of the pronunciation key!

Look It Up. Keep a good dictionary in the house. Have your child keep a list of words she does not know in the books she is reading, and have her look up each of these words. If your child asks you about a word, don't be afraid to say, "Look it up." Helping your child to look up these words will assist her in becoming an efficient dictionary user.

What Tests May Ask

Standardized tests may present a sample dictionary page and ask students a wide variety of questions about that page. This tests the child's ability to understand the parts of a dictionary and how to use them to locate words and information about those words.

Practice Skill: Dictionaries

Directions: Choose the word that would appear on a page with the pair of guide words given in the question.

Example:

pet/piece

  Ⓐ peace   Ⓑ pit

  Ⓒ pick   Ⓓ police

Answer:

  ©   pick

---

9   computer/conduct

  (A)   concise

  (B)   conference

  (C)   common

  (D)   compare

---

10   about/acorn

  (A)   also

  (B)   actor

  (C)   about

  (D)   admire

---

11   magazine/mesa

  (A)   met

  (B)   mess

  (C)   mister

  (D)   megabyte

Directions: Use the sample dictionary page to answer the following questions.

12   Which word appears last on this dictionary page?

  (A)   loom

  (B)   lunar

  (C)   luke

  (D)   lulu

---

loom * lulu

^{1}**loom** \ˈlüm\ *n* **1:** A weaving machine for making cloth   **2:** the art of weaving   **3:** the center part of an oar

^{2}**loom** \ˈlüm\ *v* **1:** to be an errie presence   **2:** to show through fog

luge (ˈlüzh) *n* **1:** one- or two-person sled for racing   **2:** a winter sport in the Olympics

luke·warm \ˈlük-ˈwȯrm\ *adj* **1:** not warm or cold in temperature <*Her bath was not too hot; it was **lukewarm.**>   **2:** showing little emotion

lu·lu \ˈlü-(ˌ)lü\ *n* [prob. fr. *Lulu,* nickname fr. *Louise*] slang : one that is remarkable or wonderful

---

13   Which word has more than one entry on the page?

  (A)   loyal   (B)   lull

  (C)   luge   (D)   loom

---

14   Which sentence uses the first definition of **lukewarm**?

  (A)   Melissa was **lukewarm** about going to the mall after dinner.

  (B)   Johanna made sure the soup was **lukewarm** for the boys.

  (C)   Have you ever known anyone to be **lukewarm** about Christmas?

  (D)   Ms. Smith's face was emotionless or **lukewarm** at the end of the day.

15 Which word below has the same vowel sound as **loom**?

(A) rue

(B) look

(C) us

(D) about

---

16 Which pair of words are the guidewords for this page?

(A) loom/loyal

(B) loom/lulu

(C) luge/lull

(D) loyal/lull

(See page 110 for the answer key.)

Parts of a Book

On the first day of school when the books are handed out, students eagerly flip through the pages to find out what they will be learning that year. Some students start at the table of contents, while others just flip at random through the chapters. Learning to use all the resources found in these books is an adventure in itself.

In an effort to help students find the information they need, textbooks published today are "student friendly," with extensive glossaries, indexes, and handbook sections.

What Fourth Graders Should Know

Students need to be familiar with the following parts of a book and how to use them:

• Table of contents
• Index
• Glossary
• References

What You and Your Child Can Do

Family Vacations. When you plan your family vacation, have your children learn a little about where they are going and what they will see before you go. Provide a variety of reference books such as atlases and encyclopedias to help.

Homework Help. During homework sessions, when your child comes to you saying "I can't find it. It's not here. I looked," don't jump to find the answer. Instead, help your child find the answer using the index and glossary of the textbook he's working with.

Writing Your Own Book. Reinforce the knowledge your child has about different parts of a book by helping her make her own, complete with table of contents and index. Have her number the pages so that it will be possible to create an index.

What Tests May Ask

Standardized tests will include a few questions about where to find information in a typical book. The tests may ask where to find a specific type of information and offer a list of possible choices, or they may provide a part of a book and ask students to define it.

Practice Skill: Parts of a Book

A Kid's Guide to Raising Dogs

by Dave Callahan

Table of Contents

Directions: Using the table of contents above, answer the following questions.

17 In which chapter would you find information about taking your dog on an airplane?

Ⓐ Chapter 2

Ⓑ Chapter 6

Ⓒ Chapter 7

Ⓓ Chapter 8

18 Where might you find information about adding a second dog to your family?

Ⓐ Chapter 1

Ⓑ Chapter 3

Ⓒ Chapter 5

Ⓓ Chapter 9

19 Where would you look for the definition of **crate training**?

Ⓐ glossary Ⓑ index

Ⓒ introduction Ⓓ Chapter 1

20 Where would you look to find out what kind of dogs are good with small children?

Ⓐ Chapter 1

Ⓑ Chapter 2

Ⓒ Chapter 3

Ⓓ Chapter 4

21 Where would you find out what this book is about?

Ⓐ introduction

Ⓑ glossary

Ⓒ index

Ⓓ Chapter 1

22 Who is the author of the book?

Ⓐ Dawna Callahan

Ⓑ Dr. Jones

Ⓒ Dave Callahan

Ⓓ Eavander Callahan

23 On what page would you find the introduction?

Ⓐ 11

Ⓑ X

Ⓒ 86

Ⓓ 90

(See page 110 for the answer key.)

Reference Books

As children progress through elementary grades, they work with not just dictionaries but also a wide variety of other resource books, such as encyclopedias, atlases, and the thesaurus.

What Fourth Graders Should Know

In the fourth grade, students are expected to complete research reports about people, places, and events using a wide variety of resources such as encyclopedias, atlases, and the thesaurus.

What You and Your Child Can Do

Organize a Home Library. Make sure your home has reference materials. Your home library should have a dictionary, thesaurus, and an atlas. It would be great if you had an almanac available as well.

Use the Phone Book. When your child wants to find out the hours of the skating rink or movie theater, have her use the phone book. Teach her how it can give more information than just the phone number.

Plan Your Family Vacation. Decide where your family will travel for vacation this year. Make a preliminary list of places to go, and then research them using an atlas, encyclopedia, and travel books.

Write School Reports. Help your child to use the wide variety of resources available to learn about the topics she is studying. If your child is learning about the respiratory system in science, enrich that study with further information from other resources.

What Tests May Ask

Standardized tests in fourth grade may include a few questions about reference books, asking students to decide which source they should go to for specific information. Many standardized tests also assess whether students know what resources to use and what information each resource provides.

Practice Skill: Reference Books

Directions: Read the following questions and choose the correct answer.

24 Where would you look to find a lot of information on the life of President James Madison?

Ⓐ dictionary

Ⓑ encyclopedia

Ⓒ atlas

Ⓓ thesaurus

25 Which heading would you look under to find information about natural resources in Utah?

Ⓐ coal

Ⓑ oil

Ⓒ Utah, Natural Resources

Ⓓ water

26 Where would you look to find a contour map of Utah?

Ⓐ dictionary   Ⓑ atlas

Ⓒ thesaurus   Ⓓ comic book

Directions: Use the map below to answer the following questions.

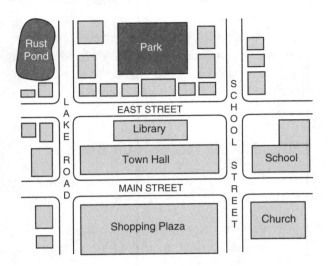

27 Which street is Rust Pond on?

    Ⓐ East Street   Ⓑ Main Street

    Ⓒ School Street   Ⓓ Lake Road

---

28 Which street corner is the church on?

    Ⓐ Main Street and School Street

    Ⓑ Main Street and Lake Road

    Ⓒ East Street and Lake Road

    Ⓓ East Street and School Street

---

29 How many houses are across from the park on School Street?

    Ⓐ 5   Ⓑ 3

    Ⓒ 2   Ⓓ 8

---

30 What building is behind the town hall on East Street?

    Ⓐ school   Ⓑ church

    Ⓒ library   Ⓓ shopping plaza

(See page 110 for the answer key.)

Charts and Graphs

Charts and graphs are typically covered in mathematics, but they are also an important component of study skills and reference books. In order to interpret many types of information, children must be able to understand a variety of charts, graphs, and maps.

What Fourth Graders Should Know

Students in fourth grade are expected to be able to read and interpret information from many types of charts and graphs, and they should be able to use these tools independently.

What You and Your Child Can Do

Plan TV Time. Sit down with your child and use the television guide to plan together what she will watch that night. Help her to understand what all the symbols mean.

Dinner Out. When you go out to a restaurant, make sure your child looks over the regular menu—not just the single-sheet kiddie list. Help your child notice what is included with each meal, and look at the different types of food. Discuss what different symbols mean (a heart may indicate a low-fat dish or a chili pepper could indicate spicy food).

Create Holiday Menus. For special dinners, have your child make a menu listing different appetizers, main courses, side dishes, desserts, and so on. Let her create a chart and decorate it when it is finished.

What Tests May Ask

Standardized tests use charts and graphs in both reading and math sections. Unfortunately, in many cases children have never seen a television guide, much less tried to use one—or they have never looked at a full restaurant menu. When children are faced with these kinds of charts in a testing situation, the first thing they do is raise their hand to ask for help—and the teacher can't help them.

Practice Skill: Charts and Graphs

Directions: Use the following menu to answer the questions.

Sensational Soups

All soups are $1.75 a cup and $2.25 a bowl.

Tomato Basil   **Carrot**
Meatball   **Turkey**
     Chicken Noodle

Super Salads

Salads are served with dressings on the side. Side salads are $.99 with a meal and $1.25 alone.

Garden salad
Iceberg lettuce, garden fresh tomatoes, cucumbers, croutons

Pasta salad
Bow tie pasta served with Romaine lettuce, broccoli, kidney beans, carrots, onions, a touch of garlic seasoned with vinaigrette dressing and parmesan cheese

Caesar salad
Fresh Romaine lettuce, croutons, fresh parmesan cheese, tossed with Caesar dressing

Available salad dressings: Ranch, Peppercorn, Italian, Light Italian, Balsamic Vinaigrette

Main Dishes

Each main dish is served with choice of vegetable and potato or rice pilaf. Add a salad for just $.99.

Chicken Parmesan--two chicken breasts, breaded and topped with marinara sauce and mozzarella cheese. Served on your choice of pasta, spaghetti, or linguini. $8.99

Marinated Sirloin Tips--tender steak tips marinated in our secret marinade and cooked on the grill to perfection. $10.99

Baked Haddock--seasoned with bread crumbs and baked until it's moist and flaky. Served with a twist of lemon. $12.99

Pasta Primavera--This special dish is for our vegetarian customers. Steamed seasonal vegetables served with angel hair pasta with primavera sauce. $7.99

Delicious Desserts

Hot fudge sundae--vanilla ice cream topped with hot fudge and whipped cream. $.99

Mom's homemade apple pie--just the way Mom makes it. Served with a scoop of vanilla ice cream. $2.99

Strawberry shortcake--fresh strawberries atop a homemade biscuit with fresh whipped cream. $2.99

Kid's Stuff

All American Hot Dog--an all-beef frank served on a toasted roll, ketchup and mustard on the side. Served with choice of chips or French fries. $2.49

Hamburger just the way you like it--an all-beef hamburger served the way you want it. Served with your choice of chips or French fries. $3.49

31 Which of the following is not a **main dish**?

  Ⓐ Caesar salad

  Ⓑ baked haddock

  Ⓒ marinated sirloin tips

  Ⓓ pasta primavera

32 Which dessert is **not** on the menu?

  Ⓐ strawberry shortcake

  Ⓑ Mom's homemade apple pie

  Ⓒ brownie sundae

  Ⓓ hot fudge sundae

33 How much is a salad with a meal?

  Ⓐ $2.49   Ⓑ $0.99

  Ⓒ $1.99   Ⓓ $0.49

34 Which meal is served exactly the way you like it?

  Ⓐ pasta primavera

  Ⓑ all American hot dog

  Ⓒ hamburger

  Ⓓ garden salad

35 Which main dish is the least expensive?

  Ⓐ chicken parmesan

  Ⓑ marinated sirloin tips

  Ⓒ baked haddock

  Ⓓ pasta primavera

(See page 110 for the answer key.)

Web Sites and Resources for More Information

Homework

Homework Central
http://www.HomeworkCentral.com
Terrific site for students, parents, and teachers, filled with information, projects, and more.

Win the Homework Wars
(Sylvan Learning Centers)
http://www.educate.com/online/qa_peters.html

Reading and Grammar Help

Born to Read: How to Raise a Reader
http://www.ala.org/alsc/raise_a_reader.html

Guide to Grammar and Writing
http://webster.commnet.edu/hp/pages/darling/grammar.htm
Help with "plague words and phrases," grammar FAQs, sentence parts, punctuation, rules for common usage.

Internet Public Library: Reading Zone
http://www.ipl.org/cgi-bin/youth/youth.out

Keeping Kids Reading and Writing
http://www.tiac.net/users/maryl/

U.S. Dept. of Education: Helping Your Child Learn to Read
http://www.ed.gov/pubs/parents/Reading/index.html

Math Help

Center for Advancement of Learning
http://www.muskingum.edu/%7Ecal/database/Math2.html
Substitution and memory strategies for math.

Center for Advancement of Learning
http://www.muskingum.edu/%7Ecal/database/Math1.html
General tips and suggestions.

Math.com
http://www.math.com
The world of math online.

Math.com
http://www.math.com/student/testprep.html
Get ready for standardized tests.

Math.com: Homework Help in Math
http://www.math.com/students/homework.html

Math.com: Math for Homeschoolers
http://www.math.com/parents/homeschool.html

The Math Forum: Problems and Puzzles
http://forum.swarthmore.edu/library/resource_types/problems_puzzles
Lots of fun math puzzles and problems for grades K through 12.

The Math Forum: Math Tips and Tricks
http://forum.swarthmore.edu/k12/mathtips/mathtips.html

Tips on Testing

Books on Test Preparation

http://www.testbooksonline.com/preHS.asp
This site provides printed resources for parents who wish to help their children prepare for standardized school tests.

Core Knowledge Web Site

http://www.coreknowledge.org/
Site dedicated to providing resources for parents; based on the books of E. D. Hirsch, Jr., who wrote the *What Your X Grader Needs to Know* series.

Family Education Network

http://www.familyeducation.com/article/0,1120,
1-6219,00.html
This report presents some of the arguments against current standardized testing practices in the public schools. The site also provides links to family activities that help kids learn.

Math.com

http://www.math.com/students/testprep.html
Get ready for standardized tests.

Standardized Tests

http://arc.missouri.edu/k12/
K through 12 assessment tools and know-how.

Parents: Testing in Schools

KidSource: Talking to Your Child's Teacher about Standardized Tests

http://www.kidsource.com/kidsource/content2/
talking.assessment.k12.4.html
This site provides basic information to help parents understand their children's test results and provides pointers for how to discuss the results with their children's teachers.

eSCORE.com: State Test and Education Standards

http://www.eSCORE.com
Find out if your child meets the necessary requirements for your local schools. A Web site with experts from Brazelton Institute and Harvard's Project Zero.

Overview of States' Assessment Programs

http://ericae.net/faqs/

Parent Soup
Education Central: Standardized Tests

http://www.parentsoup.com/edcentral/testing
A parent's guide to standardized testing in the schools, written from a parent advocacy standpoint.

National Center for Fair and Open Testing, Inc. (FairTest)

342 Broadway
Cambridge, MA 02139
(617) 864-4810
http://www.fairtest.org

National Parent Information Network

http://npin.org

Publications for Parents from the U.S. Department of Education

http://www.ed.gov/pubs/parents/
An ever-changing list of information for parents available from the U.S. Department of Education.

State of the States Report

http://www.edweek.org/sreports/qc99/states/
indicators/in-intro.htm
A report on testing and achievement in the 50 states.

Testing: General Information

Academic Center for Excellence

http://www.acekids.com

American Association for Higher Education Assessment

http://www.aahe.org/assessment/web.htm

American Educational Research Association (AERA)

http://aera.net
An excellent link to reports on American education, including reports on the controversy over standardized testing.

American Federation of Teachers

555 New Jersey Avenue, NW
Washington, D.C. 20011

Association of Test Publishers Member Products and Services
http://www.testpublishers.org/memserv.htm

Education Week on the Web
http://www.edweek.org

ERIC Clearinghouse on Assessment and Evaluation
1131 Shriver Lab
University of Maryland
College Park, MD 20742
http://ericae.net
A clearinghouse of information on assessment and education reform.

FairTest: The National Center for Fair and Open Testing
http://fairtest.org/facts/ntfact.htm
http://fairtest.org/
The National Center for Fair and Open Testing is an advocacy organization working to end the abuses, misuses, and flaws of standardized testing and to ensure that evaluation of students and workers is fair, open, and educationally sound. This site provides many links to fact sheets, opinion papers, and other sources of information about testing.

National Congress of Parents and Teachers
700 North Rush Street
Chicago, Illinois 60611

National Education Association
1201 16th Street, NW
Washington, DC 20036

National School Boards Association
http://www.nsba.org
A good source for information on all aspects of public education, including standardized testing.

Testing Our Children: A Report Card on State Assessment Systems
http://www.fairtest.org/states/survey.htm
Report of testing practices of the states, with graphical links to the states and a critique of fair testing practices in each state.

Trends in Statewide Student Assessment Programs: A Graphical Summary
http://www.ccsso.org/survey96.html
Results of annual survey of states' departments of public instruction regarding their testing practices.

U.S. Department of Education
http://www.ed.gov/

Web Links for Parents Who Want to Help Their Children Achieve
http://www.liveandlearn.com/learn.html
This page offers many Web links to free and for-sale information and materials for parents who want to help their children do well in school. Titles include such free offerings as the Online Colors Game and questionnaires to determine whether your child is ready for school.

What Should Parents Know about Standardized Testing in the Schools?
http://www.rusd.k12.ca.us/parents/standard.html
An online brochure about standardized testing in the schools, with advice regarding how to become an effective advocate for your child.

Test Publishers Online

ACT: Information for Life's Transitions
http://www.act.org

American Guidance Service, Inc.
http://www.agsnet.com

Ballard & Tighe Publishers
http://www.ballard-tighe.com

Consulting Psychologists Press
http://www.cpp-db.com

CTB McGraw-Hill
http://www.ctb.com

Educational Records Bureau
http://www.erbtest.org/index.html

Educational Testing Service
http://www.ets.org

General Educational Development (GED) Testing Service
http://www.acenet.edu/calec/ged/home.html

Harcourt Brace Educational Measurement
http://www.hbem.com

Piney Mountain Press—A Cyber-Center for Career and Applied Learning
http://www.pineymountain.com

ProEd Publishing
http://www.proedinc.com

Riverside Publishing Company
http://www.hmco.com/hmco/riverside

Stoelting Co.
http://www.stoeltingco.com

Sylvan Learning Systems, Inc.
http://www.educate.com

Touchstone Applied Science Associates, Inc. (TASA)
http://www.tasa.com

Tests Online

(*Note:* We don't endorse tests; some may not have technical documentation. Evaluate the quality of any testing program before making decisions based on its use.)

Edutest, Inc.
http://www.edutest.com
Edutest is an Internet-accessible testing service that offers criterion-referenced tests for elementary school students, based upon the standards for K through 12 learning and achievement in the states of Virginia, California, and Florida.

Virtual Knowledge
http://www.smarterkids.com
This commercial service, which enjoys a formal partnership with Sylvan Learning Centers, offers a line of skills assessments for preschool through grade 9 for use in the classroom or the home. For free online sample tests, see the Virtual Test Center.

Read More about It

Abbamont, Gary W. *Test Smart: Ready-to-Use Test-Taking Strategies and Activities for Grades 5–12.* Upper Saddle River, NJ: Prentice Hall Direct, 1997.

Cookson, Peter W., and Joshua Halberstam. *A Parent's Guide to Standardized Tests in School: How to Improve Your Child's Chances for Success.* New York: Learning Express, 1998.

Frank, Steven, and Stephen Frank. *Test-Taking Secrets: Study Better, Test Smarter, and Get Great Grades (The Backpack Study Series).* Holbrook, MA: Adams Media Corporation, 1998.

Gilbert, Sara Dulaney. *How to Do Your Best on Tests: A Survival Guide.* New York: Beech Tree Books, 1998.

Gruber, Gary. *Dr. Gary Gruber's Essential Guide to Test-Taking for Kids, Grades 3–5.* New York: William Morrow & Co., 1986.

———. *Gary Gruber's Essential Guide to Test-Taking for Kids, Grades 6, 7, 8, 9.* New York: William Morrow & Co., 1997.

Leonhardt, Mary. *99 Ways to Get Kids to Love Reading and 100 Books They'll Love.* New York: Crown, 1997.

———. *Parents Who Love Reading, Kids Who Don't: How It Happens and What You Can Do about It.* New York: Crown, 1995.

McGrath, Barbara B. *The Baseball Counting Book.* Watertown, MA: Charlesbridge, 1999.

———. *More M&M's Brand Chocolate Candies Math.* Watertown, MA: Charlesbridge, 1998.

Mokros, Janice R. *Beyond Facts & Flashcards: Exploring Math with Your Kids.* Portsmouth, NH: Heinemann, 1996.

Romain, Trevor, and Elizabeth Verdick. *True or False?: Tests Stink!* Minneapolis: Free Spirit Publishing Co., 1999.

Schartz, Eugene M. *How to Double Your Child's Grades in School: Build Brilliance and Leadership into Your Child—from Kindergarten to College—in Just 5 Minutes a Day.* New York: Barnes & Noble, 1999.

Taylor, Kathe, and Sherry Walton. *Children at the Center: A Workshop Approach to Standardized Test Preparation, K–8.* Portsmouth, NH: Heinemann, 1998.

Tobia, Sheila. *Overcoming Math Anxiety.* New York: W. W. Norton & Company, Inc., 1995.

Tufariello, Ann Hunt. *Up Your Grades: Proven Strategies for Academic Success.* Lincolnwood, IL: VGM Career Horizons, 1996.

Vorderman, Carol. *How Math Works.* Pleasantville, NY: Reader's Digest Association, Inc., 1996.

Zahler, Kathy A. *50 Simple Things You Can Do to Raise a Child Who Loves to Read.* New York: IDG Books, 1997.

What Your Child's Test Scores Mean

Several weeks or months after your child has taken standardized tests, you will receive a report such as the TerraNova Home Report found in Figures 1 and 2. You will receive similar reports if your child has taken other tests. We briefly examine what information the reports include.

Look at the first page of the Home Report. Note that the chart provides labeled bars showing the child's performance. Each bar is labeled with the child's National Percentile for that skill area. When you know how to interpret them, national percentiles can be the most useful scores you encounter on reports such as this. Even when you are confronted with different tests that use different scale scores, you can always interpret percentiles the same way, regardless of the test. A percentile tells the percent of students who score at or below that level. A percentile of 25, for example, means that 25 percent of children taking the test scored at or below that score. (It also means that 75 percent of students scored above that score.) Note that the average is always at the 50th percentile.

On the right side of the graph on the first page of the report, the publisher has designated the ranges of scores that constitute average, above average, and below average. You can also use this slightly more precise key for interpreting percentiles:

PERCENTILE RANGE	LEVEL
2 and Below	Deficient
3–8	Borderline
9–23	Low Average
24–75	Average
76–97	High Average
98 and Up	Superior

The second page of the Home report provides a listing of the child's strengths and weaknesses, along with keys for mastery, partial mastery, and non-mastery of the skills. Scoring services determine these breakdowns based on the child's scores as compared with those from the national norm group.

Your child's teacher or guidance counselor will probably also receive a profile report similar to the TerraNova Individual Profile Report, shown in Figures 3 and 4. That report will be kept in your child's permanent record. The first aspect of this report to notice is that the scores are expressed both numerically and graphically.

First look at the score bands under National Percentile. Note that the scores are expressed as bands, with the actual score represented by a dot within each band. The reason we express the scores as bands is to provide an idea of the amount by which typical scores may vary for each student. That is, each band represents a

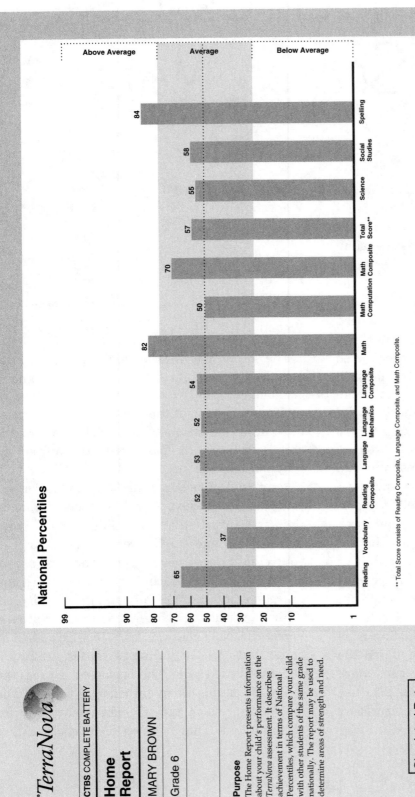

Figure 1 (SOURCE: CTB/McGraw-Hill, copyright © 1997. All rights reserved. Reproduced with permission.)

TerraNova

CTBS COMPLETE BATTERY

Home
Report

MARY BROWN

Grade 6

Purpose

This page of the Home Report presents information about your child's strengths and needs. This information is provided to help you monitor your child's academic growth.

Simulated Data

Birthdate: 02/08/85
Special Codes:
A B C D E F G H I J K L M N O P Q R S T
3 5 9 7 3 2   1 1 1
Form/Level: A-16
Test Date: 11/01/99   Scoring: PATTERN (IRT)
QM: 08   Norms Date: 1996

Class: PARKER
School: WINFIELD
District: WINFIELD

City/State: WINFIELD, CA

CTB
McGraw-Hill

Page 2   Copyright © 1997 CTB/McGraw-Hill. All rights reserved.

Strengths

Reading
● Basic Understanding
● Analyze Text

Vocabulary
● Word Meaning
● Words in Context

Language
● Editing Skills
● Sentence Structure

Language Mechanics
● Sentences, Phrases, Clauses

Mathematics
● Computation and Numerical Estimation
● Operation Concepts

Mathematics Computation
● Add Whole Numbers
● Multiply Whole Numbers

Science
● Life Science
● Inquiry Skills

Social Studies
● Geographic Perspectives
● Economic Perspectives

Spelling
● Vowels
● Consonants

Key ● Mastery

General Interpretation

The left column shows your child's best areas of performance. In each case, your child has reached mastery level. The column at the right shows the areas within each test section where your child's scores are the lowest. In these cases, your child has not reached mastery level, although he or she may have reached partial mastery.

Needs

Reading
◑ Evaluate and Extend Meaning
○ Identify Reading Strategies

Vocabulary
○ Multimeaning Words

Language
◑ Writing Strategies

Language Mechanics
○ Writing Conventions

Mathematics
◑ Measurement
◑ Geometry and Spatial Sense

Mathematics Computation
○ Percents

Science
○ Earth and Space Science

Social Studies
◑ Historical and Cultural Perspectives

Spelling
No area of needs were identified for this content area

Key ◑ Partial Mastery   ○ Non-Mastery

Figure 2   (SOURCE: CTB/McGraw-Hill, copyright © 1997. All rights reserved. Reproduced with permission.)

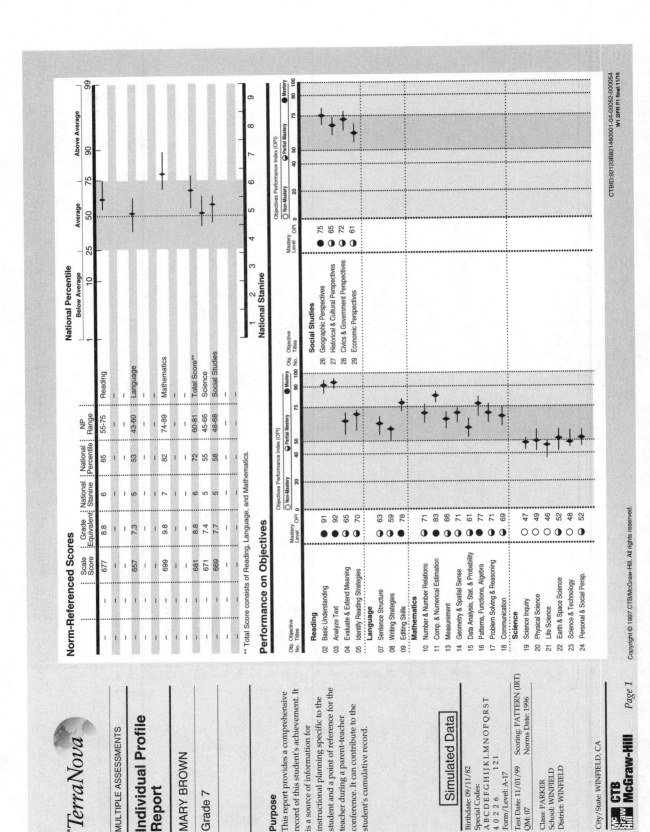

Figure 3 (SOURCE: CTB/McGraw-Hill, copyright © 1997. All rights reserved. Reproduced with permission.)

Observations

Norm-Referenced Scores

The top section of the report presents information about this student's achievement in several different ways. The National Percentile (NP) data and graph indicate how this student performed compared to students of the same grade nationally. The National Percentile range indicates that if this student had taken the test numerous times the scores would have fallen within the range shown. The shaded area on the graph represents the average range of scores, usually defined as the middle 50 percent of students nationally. Scores in the area to the right of the shading are above the average range. Scores in the area to the left of the shading are below the average range.

In Reading, for example, this student achieved a National Percentile rank of 65. This student scored higher than 65 percent of the students nationally. This score is in the average range. This student has a total of five scores in the average range. One score is in the above average range. No scores are in the below average range.

Performance on Objectives

The next section of the report presents performance on the objectives. Each objective is measured by a minimum of 4 items. The Objectives Performance Index (OPI) provides an estimate of the number of items that a student could be expected to answer correctly if there had been 100 items for that objective. The OPI is used to indicate mastery of each objective. An OPI of 75 and above characterizes Mastery. An OPI between 50 and 74 indicates Partial Mastery, and an OPI below 50 indicates Non-Mastery. The two-digit number preceding the objective title identifies the objective, which is fully described in the Teacher's Guide to *TerraNova*. The bands on either side of the diamonds indicate the range within which the student's test scores would fall if the student were tested numerous times.

In Reading, for example, this student could be expected to respond correctly to 91 out of 100 items measuring Basic Understanding. If this student had taken the test numerous times the OPI for this objective would have fallen between 82 and 93.

Teacher Notes

_____

_____

_____

_____

_____

TerraNova

MULTIPLE ASSESSMENTS

Individual Profile Report

MARY BROWN

Grade 7

Purpose

The Observations section of the Individual Profile Report gives teachers and parents information to interpret this report. This page is a narrative description of the data on the other side.

Simulated Data

Birthdate: 09/11/82
Special Codes:
A B C D E F G H I J K L M N O P Q R S T
4 0 2 2 6   1 2 1
Form/Level: A-17

Test Date: 11/01/99   Scoring: PATTERN (IRT)
QM: 08   Norms Date: 1996

Class: PARKER
School: WINFIELD
District: WINFIELD

City/State: WINFIELD, CA

CTB McGraw-Hill   *Page 2*

Figure 4

TerraNova

MULTIPLE ASSESSMENTS

Student Performance Level Report

KEN ALLEN

Grade 4

Purpose

This report describes this student's achievement in terms of five performance levels for each content area. The meaning of these levels is described on the back of this page. Performance levels are a new way of describing achievement.

Simulated Data

Birthdate: 02/08/86
Special Codes:
A B C D E F G H I J K L M N O P Q R S T
3 5 9 7 3 2   1 1 1
Form/Level: A-14
Test Date: 04/15/97   Scoring: PATTERN (IRT)
QM: 31   Norms Date: 1996

Class: SCHWARZ
School: WINFIELD
District: GREEN VALLEY

City/State: WINFIELD, CA

Performance Levels	Reading	Language	Mathematics	Science	Social Studies
5 Advanced					
4 Proficient	✓				
3 Nearing Proficiency	✓	✓	✓	✓	✓
2 Progressing	✓	✓	✓	✓	✓
1 Step 1	✓	✓	✓	✓	✓

Partially Proficient

Observations

Performance level scores provide a measure of what students *can do* in terms of the content and skills assessed by *TerraNova*, and typically found in curricula for Grades 3, 4, and 5. It is desirable to work towards achieving a Level 4 (Proficient) or Level 5 (Advanced) by the end of Grade 5.

The number of check marks indicates the performance level this student reached in each content area. For example, this student reached Level 3 in Reading and Social Studies.

The performance level indicates this student can perform the majority of what is described for that level and even more of what is described for the levels below. The student may also be capable of performing some of the things described in the next higher level, but not enough to have reached that level of performance.

For example, this student can perform the majority of what is described for Level 3 in Reading and even more of what is described for Level 2 and Level 1 in Reading. This student may also be capable of performing some of what is described for Level 4 in Reading.

For each content area look at the skills and knowledge described in the next higher level. These are the competencies this student needs to demonstrate to show academic growth.

CTB McGraw-Hill   *Page 1*

CTBID:92123B8214600001-04-00052-000054
W1 SPLR P1 final:11/09

Figure 5

Performance Levels (Grades 3, 4, 5)	Reading	Language	Mathematics	Science	Social Studies
5 Advanced	Students use analogies to generalize. They identify a paraphrase of concepts or ideas in texts. They can indicate thought processes that led them to a previous answer. In written responses, they demonstrate understanding of an implied theme, assess intent of passage information, and provide justification as well as support for their answers.	Students understand logical development in paragraph structure. They identify essential information from notes. They recognize the effect of prepositional phrases on subject-verb agreement. They find and correct at least 4 out of 6 errors when editing simple narratives. They correct run-on and incomplete sentences in more complex texts. They can eliminate all errors while editing their own work.	Students locate decimals on a number line; compute with decimals and fractions; read scale drawings; find areas; identify geometric transformations; construct and label bar graphs; find simple probabilities; find averages; use patterns in data to solve problems; use multiple strategies and concepts to solve unfamiliar problems; express mathematical ideas and explain the problem-solving process.	Students understand a broad range of grade level scientific concepts, such as the structure of Earth and instinctive behavior. They know terminology, such as decomposers, fossil fuel, eclipse, and buoyancy. Knowledge of more complex environmental issues includes, for example, the positive consequences of a forest fire. Students can process and interpret more detailed tables and graphs. They can suggest improvements to experimental design, such as running more trials.	Students consistently demonstrate skills such as synthesizing information from two sources (e.g., a document and a map). They show understanding of the democratic process and global environmental issues, and know the location of continents and major countries. They analyze and summarize information from multiple sources in early American history. They thoroughly explain both sides of an issue and give complete and detailed written answers to questions.
4 Proficient	Students interpret figures of speech. They recognize paraphrase of text information and retrieve information to complete forms. In more complex texts, they identify themes, main ideas, or author purpose/point of view. They analyze and apply information in graphic and text form, make reasonable generalizations, and draw conclusions. In written responses, they can identify key elements from text.	Students select the best supporting sentences for a topic sentence. They use compound predicates to combine sentences. They identify simple subjects and predicates, recognize correct usage when confronted with two types of errors, and find and correct at least 3 out of 6 errors when editing simple narratives. They can edit their own work with only minor errors.	Students compare, order, and round whole numbers; know place value to thousands; identify fractions; use computation and estimation strategies; relate multiplication to addition; measure to nearest half-inch and centimeter; estimate and find perimeters; estimate measures; find elapsed times; combine and subdivide shapes; identify parallel lines; interpret tables and graphs; solve two-step problems.	Students have a range of specific science knowledge, including details about animal adaptations and classification, states of matter, and the geology of Earth. They recognize scientific words such as habitat, gravity, and mass. They understand the usefulness of computers. They understand reasons for conserving natural resources. Understanding of experimentation includes analyzing purpose, interpreting data, and selecting tools to gather data.	Students demonstrate skills such as making inferences, using historical documents and analyzing maps to determine the economic strengths of a region. They understand the function of currency in various cultures and supply and demand. They summarize information from multiple sources, recognize relationships, determine relevance of information, and show global awareness. They propose solutions to real-world problems and support ideas with appropriate details.
3 Nearing Proficiency	Students use context clues and structural analysis to determine word meaning. They recognize homonyms and antonyms in grade-level text. They identify important details, sequence, cause and effect, and lessons embedded in the text. They interpret characters' feelings and apply information to new situations. In written responses, they can express an opinion and support it.	Students identify irrelevant sentences in paragraphs and select the best place to insert new information. They recognize faulty sentence construction. They combine simple sentences with conjunctions. They understand the subordination of phrases/clauses. They identify reference sources. They recognize correct conventions for dates, closings, and place names in informal correspondence.	Students identify even and odd numbers; subtract whole numbers with regrouping; multiply and divide by one-digit numbers; identify simple fractions; measure with ruler to nearest inch; tell time to nearest fifteen minutes; recognize and classify common shapes; recognize symmetry; subdivide shapes; complete bar graphs; extend numerical and geometric patterns; apply simple logical reasoning.	Students are familiar with the life cycles of plants and animals. They can identify an example of a cold-blooded animal. They infer what once existed from fossil evidence. They recognize the term habitat. They understand the water cycle. They know science and society issues such as recycling and causes of pollution. They can sequence technological advances. They extrapolate data, devise a simple classification scheme, and determine the purpose of a simple experiment.	Students demonstrate skills in organizing information. They use time lines, product and global maps, and cardinal directions. They understand simple cause and effect relationships and historical documents. They sequence holidays with events, associate natural resources. They compare life in different times and understand some economic concepts related to products, jobs, and the environment. They give some detail in written responses.
2 Progressing	Students identify synonyms for grade-level words, and use context clues to define common words. They make simple inferences and predictions based on text. They identify characters' feelings. They can transfer information from text to graphic form, or from graphic form to text. In written responses, they can provide limited support for their answers.	Students identify the use of correct verb tenses and supply verbs to complete sentences. They complete paragraphs by selecting an appropriate topic sentence. They select correct adjective forms.	Students know ordinal numbers; solve coin combination problems; count by tens; add whole numbers with regrouping; have basic estimation skills; understand addition property of zero; write and identify number sentences describing simple situations; read calendars; identify appropriate measurement tools; recognize congruent figures; use simple coordinate grids; read common tables and graphs.	Students recognize that plants decompose and become part of soil. They can classify a plant as a vegetable. They recognize that camouflage relates to survival. They recognize terms such as hibernate. They have an understanding of human impact on the environment and are familiar with causes of pollution. They find the correct bar graph to represent given data and transfer data appropriate for middle elementary grades to a bar graph.	Students demonstrate simple information-processing skills such as using basic maps and keys. They recognize simple geographical terms, types of jobs, modes of transportation, and natural resources. They connect a human need with an appropriate community service. They identify some early famous presidents and know the capital of the United States. Their written answers are partially complete.
1 Step 1	Students select pictured representations of ideas and identify stated details contained in simple texts. In written responses, they can select and transfer information from charts.	Students supply subjects to complete sentences. They identify the correct use of pronouns. They edit for the correct use of end marks and initial capital letters, and identify the correct convention for greetings in letters.	Students read and recognize numbers to 1000; identify real-world use of numbers; add and subtract two-digit numbers without regrouping; identify addition situations; recognize and complete simple geometric and numerical patterns.	Students recognize basic adaptations for living in the water, identify an animal that is hatched from an egg, and associate an organism with its correct environment. They identify an object as metal. They have some understanding of conditions on the moon. They supply one way a computer can be useful. They associate an instrument like a telescope with a field of study.	Students are developing fundamental social studies skills such as locating and classifying basic information. They locate information in pictures and read and complete simple bar graphs related to social studies concepts and contexts. They can connect some city buildings with their functions and recognize certain historical objects.

(Levels 5, 4, 3 are grouped as "Proficient"; levels 2 and 1 are grouped as "Partially Proficient.")

W1 SPLR P2:11/02

IMPORTANT: Each performance level, depicted on the other side, indicates the student can perform the majority of what is described for that level and even more of what is described for the levels below. The student may also be capable of performing some of the things described in the next higher level, but not enough to have reached that level.

Figure 6

confidence interval. In these reports, we usually report either a 90 percent or 95 percent confidence interval. Interpret a confidence interval this way: Suppose we report a 90 percent confidence interval of 25 to 37. This means we estimate that, if the child took the test multiple times, we would expect that child's score to be in the 25 to 37 range 90 percent of the time.

Now look under the section titled Norm-Referenced Scores on the first page of the Individual Profile Report (Figure 3). The farthest column on the right provides the NP Range, which is the National Percentile scores represented by the score bands in the chart.

Next notice the column labeled Grade Equivalent. Theoretically, grade level equivalents equate a student's score in a skill area with the average grade placement of children who made the same score. Many psychologists and test developers would prefer that we stopped reporting grade equivalents, because they can be grossly misleading. For example, the average reading grade level of high school seniors as reported by one of the more popular tests is the eighth grade level. Does that mean that the nation's high school seniors cannot read? No. The way the test publisher calculated grade equivalents was to determine the average test scores for students in grades 4 to 6 and then simply extend the resulting prediction formula to grades 7 to 12. The result is that parents of average high school seniors who take the test in question would mistakenly believe that their seniors are reading four grade levels behind! Stick to the percentile in interpreting your child's scores.

Now look at the columns labeled Scale Score and National Stanine. These are two of a group of scores we also call *standard scores*. In reports for other tests, you may see other standard scores reported, such as Normal Curve Equivalents (NCEs), Z-Scores, and T-Scores. The IQ that we report on intelligence tests, for example, is a standard score. Standard scores are simply a way of expressing a student's scores in terms of the statistical properties of the scores from the norm group against which we are comparing the child. Although most psychologists prefer to speak in terms of standard scores among themselves, parents are advised to stick to percentiles in interpreting your child's performance.

Now look at the section of the report labeled Performance on Objectives. In this section, the test publisher reports how your child did on the various skills that make up each skills area. Note that the scores on each objective are expressed as a percentile band, and you are again told whether your child's score constitutes mastery, non-mastery, or partial mastery. Note that these scores are made up of tallies of sometimes small numbers of test items taken from sections such as Reading or Math. Because they are calculated from a much smaller number of scores than the main scales are (for example, Sentence Comprehension is made up of fewer items than overall Reading), their scores are less reliable than those of the main scales.

Now look at the second page of the Individual Profile Report (Figure 4). Here the test publisher provides a narrative summary of how the child did on the test. These summaries are computer-generated according to rules provided by the publisher. Note that the results descriptions are more general than those on the previous three report pages. But they allow the teacher to form a general picture of which students are performing at what general skill levels.

Finally, your child's guidance counselor may receive a summary report such as the TerraNova Student Performance Level Report. (See Figures 5 and 6.) In this report, the publisher explains to school personnel what skills the test assessed and generally how proficiently the child tested under each skill.

Which States Require Which Tests

Tables 1 through 3 summarize standardized testing practices in the 50 states and the District of Columbia. This information is constantly changing; the information presented here was accurate as of the date of printing of this book. Many states have changed their testing practices in response to revised accountability legislation, while others have changed the tests they use.

Table 1   State Web Sites: Education and Testing

STATE	GENERAL WEB SITE	STATE TESTING WEB SITE
Alabama	http://www.alsde.edu/	http://www.fairtest.org/states/al.htm
Alaska	www.educ.state.ak.us/	http://www.educ.state.ak.us/
Arizona	http://www.ade.state.az.us/	http://www.ade.state.az.us/standards/
Arkansas	http://arkedu.k12.ar.us/	http://www.fairtest.org/states/ar.htm
California	http://goldmine.cde.ca.gov/	http://star.cde.ca.gov/
Colorado	http://www.cde.state.co.us/index_home.htm	http://www.cde.state.co.us/index_assess.htm
Connecticut	http://www.state.ct.us/sde/	http://www.state.ct.us/sde/cmt/index.htm
Delaware	http://www.doe.state.de.us/	http://www.doe.state.de.us/aab/index.htm
District of Columbia	http://www.k12.dc.us/dcps/home.html	http://www.k12.dc.us/dcps/data/data_frame2.html
Florida	http://www.firn.edu/doe/	http://www.firn.edu/doe/sas/sasshome.htm
Georgia	http://www.doe.k12.ga.us/	http://www.doe.k12.ga.us/sla/ret/recotest.html
Hawaii	http://kalama.doe.hawaii.edu/upena/	http://www.fairtest.org/states/hi.htm
Idaho	http://www.sde.state.id.us/Dept/	http://www.sde.state.id.us/instruct/ schoolaccount/statetesting.htm
Illinois	http://www.isbe.state.il.us/	http://www.isbe.state.il.us/isat/
Indiana	http://doe.state.in.us/	http://doe.state.in.us/assessment/welcome.html
Iowa	http://www.state.ia.us/educate/index.html	(Tests Chosen Locally)
Kansas	http://www.ksbe.state.ks.us/	http://www.ksbe.state.ks.us/assessment/
Kentucky	http://www.kde.state.ky.us/	http://www.kde.state.ky.us/oaa/
Louisiana	http://www.doe.state.la.us/DOE/asps/home.asp	http://www.doe.state.la.us/DOE/asps/home.asp? I=HISTAKES
Maine	http://janus.state.me.us/education/homepage.htm	http://janus.state.me.us/education/mea/ meacompass.htm
Maryland	http://www.msde.state.md.us/	http://msp.msde.state.md.us/
Massachusetts	http://www.doe.mass.edu/	http://www.doe.mass.edu/mcas/
Michigan	http://www.mde.state.mi.us/	http://www.MeritAward.state.mi.us/merit/meap/ index.htm

STATE	GENERAL WEB SITE	STATE TESTING WEB SITE
Minnesota	http://www.educ.state.mn.us/	http://fairtest.org/states/mn.htm
Mississippi	http://mdek12.state.ms.us/	http://fairtest.org/states/ms.htm
Missouri	http://services.dese.state.mo.us/	http://fairtest.org/states/mo.htm
Montana	http://www.metnet.state.mt.us/	http://fairtest.org/states/mt.htm
Nebraska	http://www.nde.state.ne.us/	http://www.edneb.org/IPS/AppAccrd/ApprAccrd.html
Nevada	http://www.nde.state.nv.us/	http://www.nsn.k12.nv.us/nvdoe/reports/TerraNova.doc
New Hampshire	http://www.state.nh.us/doe/	http://www.state.nh.us/doe/Assessment/assessme(NHEIAP).htm
New Jersey	http://www.state.nj.us/education/	http://www.state.nj.us/njded/stass/index.html
New Mexico	http://sde.state.nm.us/	http://sde.state.nm.us/press/august30a.html
New York	http://www.nysed.gov/	http://www.emsc.nysed.gov/ciai/assess.html
North Carolina	http://www.dpi.state.nc.us/	http://www.dpi.state.nc.us/accountability/reporting/index.html
North Dakota	http://www.dpi.state.nd.us/dpi/index.htm	http://www.dpi.state.nd.us/dpi/reports/assess/assess.htm
Ohio	http://www.ode.state.oh.us/	http://www.ode.state.oh.us/ca/
Oklahoma	http://sde.state.ok.us/	http://sde.state.ok.us/acrob/testpack.pdf
Oregon	http://www.ode.state.or.us//	http://www.ode.state.or.us//asmt/index.htm
Pennsylvania	http://www.pde.psu.edu/	http://www.fairtest.org/states/pa.htm
Rhode Island	http://www.ridoe.net/	http://www.ridoe.net/standards/default.htm
South Carolina	http://www.state.sc.us/sde/	http://www.state.sc.us/sde/reports/terranov.htm
South Dakota	http://www.state.sd.us/state/executive/deca/	http://www.state.sd.us/state/executive/deca/TA/McRelReport/McRelReports.htm
Tennessee	http://www.state.tn.us/education/	http://www.state.tn.us/education/tsintro.htm
Texas	http://www.tea.state.tx.us/	http://www.tea.state.tx.us/student.assessment/
Utah	http://www.usoe.k12.ut.us/	http://www.usoe.k12.ut.us/eval/usoeeval.htm
Vermont	http://www.state.vt.us/educ/	http://www.fairtest.org/states/vt.htm

STATE	GENERAL WEB SITE	STATE TESTING WEB SITE
Virginia	http://www.pen.k12.va.us/Anthology/VDOE/	http://www.pen.k12.va.us/VDOE/Assessment/home.shtml
Washington	http://www.k12.wa.us/	http://www.k12.wa.us/assessment/
West Virginia	http://wvde.state.wv.us/	http://wvde.state.wv.us/
Wisconsin	http://www.dpi.state.wi.us/	http://www.dpi.state.wi.us/dpi/dltcl/eis/achfacts.html
Wyoming	http://www.k12.wy.us/wdehome.html	http://www.asme.com/wycas/index.htm

Table 2 Norm-Referenced and Criterion-Referenced Tests Administered by State

STATE	NORM-REFERENCED TEST	CRITERION-REFERENCED TEST	EXIT EXAM
Alabama	Stanford Achievement Test		Alabama High School Graduation Exam
Alaska	California Achievement Test	Alaska Benchmark Examinations	
Arizona	Stanford Achievement Test	Arizona's Instrument to Measure Standards (AIMS)	
Arkansas	Stanford Achievement Test		
California	Stanford Achievement Test	Standardized Testing and Reporting Supplement	High School Exit Exam (HSEE)
Colorado	None	Colorado Student Assessment Program	
Connecticut		Connecticut Mastery Test	
Delaware	Stanford Achievement Test	Delaware Student Testing Program	
District of Columbia	Stanford Achievement Test		
Florida	(Locally Selected)	Florida Comprehensive Assessment Test (FCAT)	High School Competency Test (HSCT)
Georgia	Stanford Achievement Test	Georgia Kindergarten Assessment Program—Revised and Criterion-Referenced Competency Tests (CRCT)	Georgia High School Graduation Tests
Hawaii	Stanford Achievement Test	Credit by Examination	Hawaii State Test of Essential Competencies
Idaho	Iowa Tests of Basic Skills/ Tests of Achievement and Proficiency	Direct Writing/Mathematics Assessment, Idaho Reading Indicator	
Illinois		Illinois Standards Achievement Tests	Prairie State Achievement Examination
Indiana		Indiana Statewide Testing for Educational Progress	
Iowa	(None)		
Kansas		(State-Developed Tests)	
Kentucky	Comprehensive Test of Basic Skills	Kentucky Core Content Tests	
Louisiana	Iowa Tests of Basic Skills	Louisiana Educational Assessment Program	Graduate Exit Exam
Maine		Maine Educational Assessment	High School Assessment Test
Maryland		Maryland School Performance Assessment Program, Maryland Functional Testing Program	

STATE	NORM-REFERENCED TEST	CRITERION-REFERENCED TEST	EXIT EXAM
Massachusetts		Massachusetts Comprehensive Assessment System	
Michigan		Michigan Educational Assessment Program	High School Test
Minnesota		Basic Standards Test	Profile of Learning
Mississippi	Comprehensive Test of Basic Skills	Subject Area Testing Program	Functional Literacy Examination
Missouri		Missouri Mastery and Achievement Test	
Montana	Iowa Tests of Basic Skills		
Nebraska			
Nevada	TerraNova		Nevada High School Proficiency Examination
New Hampshire		NH Educational Improvement and Assessment Program	
New Jersey		Elementary School Proficiency Test/Early Warning Test	High School Proficiency Test
New Mexico	TerraNova		New Mexico High School Competency Exam
New York		Pupil Evaluation Program/ Preliminary Competency Tests	Regents Competency Tests
North Carolina	Iowa Tests of Basic Skills	NC End of Grade Test	
North Dakota	TerraNova	ND Reading, Writing, Speaking, Listening, Math Test	
Ohio		Ohio Proficiency Tests	Ohio Proficiency Tests
Oklahoma	Iowa Tests of Basic Skills	Oklahoma Criterion-Referenced Tests	
Oregon		Oregon Statewide Assessment	
Pennsylvania		Pennsylvania System of School Assessment	
Rhode Island	Metropolitan Achievement Test	New Standards English Language Arts Reference Exam, New Standards Mathematics Reference Exam, Rhode Island Writing Assessment, and Rhode Island Health Education Assessment	
South Carolina	TerraNova	Palmetto Achievement Challenge Tests	High School Exit Exam
South Dakota	Stanford Achievement Test		
Tennessee	Tennessee Comprehensive Assessment Program	Tennessee Comprehensive Assessment Program	

STATE	NORM-REFERENCED TEST	CRITERION-REFERENCED TEST	EXIT EXAM
Texas		Texas Assessment of Academic Skills, End-of-Course Examinations	Texas Assessment of Academic Skills
Utah	Stanford Achievement Test	Core Curriculum Testing	
Vermont		New Standards Reference Exams	
Virginia	Stanford Achievement Test	Virginia Standards of Learning	Virginia Standards of Learning
Washington	Iowa Tests of Basic Skills	Washington Assessment of Student Learning	Washington Assessment of Student Learning
West Virginia	Stanford Achievement Test		
Wisconsin	TerraNova	Wisconsin Knowledge and Concepts Examinations	
Wyoming	TerraNova	Wyoming Comprehensive Assessment System	Wyoming Comprehensive Assessment System

Table 3 Standardized Test Schedules by State

STATE	KG	1	2	3	4	5	6	7	8	9	10	11	12	COMMENT
Alabama				X	X	X	X	X	X	X	X	X	X	
Alaska				X	X		X		X			X		
Arizona			X	X	X	X	X	X	X	X	X	X	X	
Arkansas					X	X		X	X		X	X	X	
California			X	X	X	X	X	X	X	X	X	X		
Colorado				X	X	X		X	X					
Connecticut					X		X		X					
Delaware				X	X	X			X		X	X		
District of Columbia		X	X	X	X	X	X	X	X	X	X	X		
Florida				X	X	X			X		X			There is no state-mandated norm-referenced testing. However, the state collects information furnished by local districts that elect to perform norm-referenced testing. The FCAT is administered to Grades 4, 8, and 10 to assess reading and Grades 5, 8, and 10 to assess math.
Georgia	X			X	X	X	X		X			X		
Hawaii				X			X		X		X			The Credit by Examination is voluntary and is given in Grade 8 in Algebra and Foreign Languages.
Idaho				X	X	X	X	X	X	X	X	X		
Illinois				X	X	X		X	X		X	X		Exit Exam failure will not disqualify students from graduation if all other requirements are met.
Indiana				X			X		X		X			
Iowa		*	*	*	*	*	*	*	*	*	*	*	*	*Iowa does not currently have a statewide testing program. Locally chosen assessments are administered to grades determined locally.
Kansas				X	X	X		X	X		X	X		

STATE	KG	1	2	3	4	5	6	7	8	9	10	11	12	COMMENT
Kentucky					X	X	X	X	X	X	X	X	X	
Louisiana				X	X	X	X	X	X	X	X	X	X	
Maine					X					X			X		
Maryland				X		X			X	X	X	X	X	
Massachusetts				X	X	X		X	X	X	X			
Michigan					X	X		X	X					
Minnesota				X		X			X	X	X	X	X	
Mississippi				X	X	X	X	X	X					Mississippi officials would not return phone calls or emails regarding this information.
Missouri		X	X	X	X	X	X	X	X	X	X			
Montana					X				X		X			The State Board of Education has decided to use a single norm-referenced test statewide beginning 2000–2001 school year.
Nebraska		**	**	**	**	**	**	**	**	**	**	**	**	**Decisions regarding testing are left to the individual school districts.
Nevada					X				X					Districts choose whether and how to test with norm-referenced tests.
New Hampshire				X			X				X			
New Jersey				X	X			X	X	X	X	X		
New Mexico					X		X		X					
New York				X	X	X	X	X	X	X			X	Assessment program is going through major revisions.
North Carolina	X			X	X	X	X		X	X			X	NRT Testing selects samples of students, not all.
North Dakota					X		X		X		X			
Ohio					X		X			X			X	
Oklahoma				X		X		X	X			X		
Oregon				X		X			X		X			

STATE	KG	1	2	3	4	5	6	7	8	9	10	11	12	COMMENT
Pennsylvania						X	X		X	X		X		
Rhode Island				X	X	X		X	X	X	X	X		
South Carolina				X	X	X	X	X	X	X	X	***	***	***Students who fail the High School Exit Exam have opportunities to take the exam again in grades 11 and 12.
South Dakota			X		X	X			X	X		X		
Tennessee			X	X	X	X	X	X	X					
Texas				X	X	X	X	X	X		X	X	X	
Utah		X	X	X	X	X	X	X	X	X	X	X	X	
Vermont					X	X	X		X	X	X	X		Rated by the Centers for Fair and Open Testing as a nearly model system for assessment.
Virginia				X	X	X	X		X	X		X		
Washington					X			X			X			
West Virginia				X	X	X	X	X	X	X	X	X		
Wisconsin					X				X		X			
Wyoming					X				X			X		

Testing Accommodations

The more testing procedures vary from one classroom or school to the next, the less we can compare the scores from one group to another. Consider a test in which the publisher recommends that three sections of the test be given in one 45-minute session per day on three consecutive days. School A follows those directions. To save time, School B gives all three sections of the test in one session lasting slightly more than two hours. We can't say that both schools followed the same testing procedures. Remember that the test publishers provide testing procedures so schools can administer the tests in as close a manner as possible to the way the tests were administered to the groups used to obtain test norms. When we compare students' scores to norms, we want to compare apples to apples, not apples to oranges.

Most schools justifiably resist making any changes in testing procedures. Informally, a teacher can make minor changes that don't alter the testing procedures, such as separating two students who talk with each other instead of paying attention to the test; letting Lisa, who is getting over an ear infection, sit closer to the front so she can hear better; or moving Jeffrey away from the window to prevent his looking out the window and daydreaming.

There are two groups of students who require more formal testing accommodations. One group of students is identified as having a disability under Section 504 of the Rehabilitation Act of 1973 (Public Law 93-112). These students face some challenge but, with reasonable and appropriate accommodation, can take advantage of the same educational opportunities as other students. That is, they have a condition that requires some accommodation for them.

Just as schools must remove physical barriers to accommodate students with disabilities, they must make appropriate accommodations to remove other types of barriers to students' access to education. Marie is profoundly deaf, even with strong hearing aids. She does well in school with the aid of an interpreter, who signs her teacher's instructions to her and tells her teacher what Marie says in reply. An appropriate accommodation for Marie would be to provide the interpreter to sign test instructions to her, or to allow her to watch a videotape with an interpreter signing test instructions. Such a reasonable accommodation would not deviate from standard testing procedures and, in fact, would ensure that Marie received the same instructions as the other students.

If your child is considered disabled and has what is generally called a Section 504 Plan or individual accommodation plan (IAP), then the appropriate way to ask for testing accommodations is to ask for them in a meeting to discuss school accommodations under the plan. If your child is not already covered by such a plan, he or she won't qualify for one merely because you request testing accommodations.

The other group of students who may receive formal testing accommodations are those identified as handicapped under the Individuals with Disabilities Education Act (IDEA)—students with mental retardation, learning disabilities, serious emotional disturbance, orthopedic handicap, hearing or visual problems, and other handicaps defined in the law. These students have been identified under procedures governed by federal and sometimes state law, and their education is governed by a document called the Individualized Educational Program (IEP). Unless you are under a court order specifically revoking your educational rights on behalf of your child, you are a full member of the IEP team even if you and your child's other parent are divorced and the other parent has custody. Until recently, IEP teams actually had the prerogative to exclude certain handicapped students from taking standardized group testing altogether. However, today states make it more difficult to exclude students from testing.

If your child is classified as handicapped and has an IEP, the appropriate place to ask for testing accommodations is in an IEP team meeting. In fact, federal regulations require IEP teams to address testing accommodations. You have the right to call a meeting at any time. In that meeting, you will have the opportunity to present your case for the accommodations you believe are necessary. Be prepared for the other team members to resist making extreme accommodations unless you can present a very strong case. If your child is identified as handicapped and you believe that he or she should be provided special testing accommodations, contact the person at your child's school who is responsible for convening IEP meetings and request a meeting to discuss testing accommodations.

Problems arise when a request is made for accommodations that cause major departures from standard testing procedures. For example, Lynn has an identified learning disability in mathematics calculation and attends resource classes for math. Her disability is so severe that her IEP calls for her to use a calculator when performing all math problems. She fully under-stands math concepts, but she simply can't perform the calculations without the aid of a calculator. Now it's time for Lynn to take the school-based standardized tests, and she asks to use a calculator. In this case, since her IEP already requires her to be provided with a calculator when performing math calculations, she may be allowed a calculator during school standardized tests. However, because using a calculator constitutes a major violation of standard testing procedures, her score on all sections in which she is allowed to use a calculator will be recorded as a failure, and her results in some states will be removed from among those of other students in her school in calculating school results.

How do we determine whether a student is allowed formal accommodations in standardized school testing and what these accommodations may be? First, if your child is not already identified as either handicapped or disabled, having the child classified in either group solely to receive testing accommodations will be considered a violation of the laws governing both classifications. Second, even if your child is already classified in either group, your state's department of public instruction will provide strict guidelines for the testing accommodations schools may make. Third, even if your child is classified in either group and you are proposing testing accommodations allowed under state testing guidelines, any accommodations must still be both *reasonable* and *appropriate*. To be reasonable and appropriate, testing accommodations must relate to your child's disability and must be similar to those already in place in his or her daily educational program. If your child is always tested individually in a separate room for all tests in all subjects, then a similar practice in taking school-based standardized tests may be appropriate. But if your child has a learning disability only in mathematics calculation, requesting that all test questions be read to him or her is inappropriate because that accommodation does not relate to his identified handicap.

Glossary

Accountability The idea that a school district is held responsible for the achievement of its students. The term may also be applied to holding students responsible for a certain level of achievement in order to be promoted or to graduate.

Achievement test An assessment that measures current knowledge in one or more of the areas taught in most schools, such as reading, math, and language arts.

Aptitude test An assessment designed to predict a student's potential for learning knowledge or skills.

Content validity The extent to which a test represents the content it is designed to cover.

Criterion-referenced test A test that rates how thoroughly a student has mastered a specific skill or area of knowledge. Typically, a criterion-referenced test is subjective, and relies on someone to observe and rate student work; it doesn't allow for easy comparisons of achievement among students. Performance assessments are criterion-referenced tests. The opposite of a criterion-referenced test is a norm-referenced test.

Frequency distribution A tabulation of individual scores (or groups of scores) that shows the number of persons who obtained each score.

Generalizability The idea that the score on a test reflects what a child knows about a subject, or how well he performs the skills the test is supposed to be assessing. Generalizability requires that enough test items are administered to truly assess a student's achievement.

Grade equivalent A score on a scale developed to indicate the school grade (usually measured in months of a year) that corresponds to an average chronological age, mental age, test score, or other characteristic. A grade equivalent of 6.4 is interpreted as a score that is average for a group in the fourth month of Grade 6.

High-stakes assessment A type of standardized test that has major consequences for a student or school (such as whether a child graduates from high school or gets admitted to college).

Mean Average score of a group of scores.

Median The middle score in a set of scores ranked from smallest to largest.

National percentile Percentile score derived from the performance of a group of individuals across the nation.

Normative sample A comparison group consisting of individuals who have taken a test under standard conditions.

Norm-referenced test A standardized test that can compare scores of students in one school with a reference group (usually other students in the same grade and age, called the "norm group"). Norm-referenced tests compare the achievement of one student or the students of a school, school district, or state with the norm score.

Norms A summary of the performance of a group of individuals on which a test was standardized.

Percentile An incorrect form of the word *centile,* which is the percent of a group of scores that falls below a given score. Although the correct term is *centile,* much of the testing literature has adopted the term *percentile.*

Performance standards A level of performance on a test set by education experts.

Quartiles Points that divide the frequency distribution of scores into equal fourths.

Regression to the mean The tendency of scores in a group of scores to vary in the direction of the mean. For example: If a child has an abnormally low score on a test, she is likely to make a higher score (that is, one closer to the mean) the next time she takes the test.

Reliability The consistency with which a test measures some trait or characteristic. A measure can be reliable without being valid, but it can't be valid without being reliable.

Standard deviation A statistical measure used to describe the extent to which scores vary in a group of scores. Approximately 68 percent of scores in a group are expected to be in a range from one standard deviation below the mean to one standard deviation above the mean.

Standardized test A test that contains well-defined questions of proven validity and that produces reliable scores. Such tests are commonly paper-and-pencil exams containing multiple-choice items, true or false questions, matching exercises, or short fill-in-the-blanks items. These tests may also include performance assessment items (such as a writing sample), but assessment items cannot be completed quickly or scored reliably.

Test anxiety Anxiety that occurs in test-taking situations. Test anxiety can seriously impair individuals' ability to obtain accurate scores on a test.

Validity The extent to which a test measures the trait or characteristic it is designed to measure. Also see *reliability.*

Answer Keys for Practice Skills

Chapter 1:
Test-Taking Basics

1 C
2 D
3 A
4 B
5 D
6 C

Chapter 2:
Vocabulary

1 B
2 C
3 C
4 A
5 B
6 A
7 B
8 D
9 A
10 A

Chapter 3:
Word Meanings in Context

1 C
2 D
3 A
4 A
5 B
6 A

7 B
8 A
9 B
10 D
11 A
12 B
13 B
14 A
15 D
16 B
17 C
18 D

Chapter 4:
Synonyms, Antonyms, and Homophones

1 A
2 C
3 D
4 B
5 A
6 D
7 C
8 B
9 A
10 A
11 B
12 A
13 B
14 B

15 A
16 B
17 B
18 C
19 C
20 D

Chapter 5:
Spelling

1 C
2 A
3 B
4 B
5 C
6 A
7 D
8 B
9 C
10 D
11 C
12 A
13 B
14 C
15 B
16 C
17 D
18 D
19 A
20 C
21 D
22 C

23 A
24 C
25 A
26 D
27 A
28 B
29 A
30 C
31 A
32 D
33 C
34 D
35 B
36 B
37 A
38 C
39 C
40 A
41 C
42 B
43 B
44 D
45 B

Chapter 6:
Grammar

1 B
2 A
3 B
4 B
5 C

6	D
7	B
8	C
9	C
10	C
11	D

Chapter 7:
Breaking It Down

1	C
2	C
3	A
4	B
5	D
6	C
7	C
8	D
9	B
10	B

Chapter 8:
Reading
Comprehension

1	A
2	B
3	B

4	C
5	B
6	A
7	C
8	D
9	C
10	D
11	A
12	A
13	D
14	B
15	C
16	B

Chapter 9:
Literary Genres

1	C
2	C
3	B
4	D
5	A
6	D
7	D
8	C
9	A
10	B

11	C
12	C
13	A
14	A
15	D
16	C
17	C
18	B
19	C
20	B
21	D

Chapter 10:
Study Skills

1	B
2	B
3	D
4	A
5	A
6	B
7	C
8	A
9	A
10	C
11	D
12	D

13	D
14	B
15	A
16	B
17	C
18	D
19	A
20	A
21	A
22	C
23	B
24	B
25	C
26	B
27	D
28	A
29	B
30	C
31	A
32	C
33	B
34	C
35	D

Sample Practice Test

You may be riding a roller coaster of feelings and opinions at this point. If your child has gone through the preceding chapters easily, then you're both probably excited to move on, to jump in with both feet, take the test, and that will be that. On the other hand, your child may have struggled a bit with some of the chapters. Some of the concepts may be difficult for him and will require a little more practice. Never fear!

All children acquire skills in all areas of learning when they are developmentally ready. We can't push them, but we can reinforce the skills that they already know. In addition, we can play games and do activities to pave the way for their understanding of the skills that they will need to master later. With luck, that's what you've done with the preceding chapters.

The test that follows is designed to incorporate components of several different kinds of standardized tests. The test that your child takes in school probably won't look just like this one, but it should be sufficiently similar that he should be pretty comfortable with the format. The administration of tests varies as well. It is important that your child hear the rhythm and language used in standardized tests. If you wish, you may have your child read the directions that precede each test section to you first and explain what the item is asking

him to do. Your child may try it on his own if you feel he understands it, or you may want to clarify the instructions.

Test Administration

If you like, you may complete the entire test in one day, but it is not recommended that your child attempt to finish it in one sitting. As test administrator, you'll find that you'll need to stretch, have a snack, or use the bathroom too! If you plan to do the test in one day, leave at least 15 minutes between sessions.

Before you start, prepare a quiet place, free of distractions. Have two or three sharpened pencils with erasers that don't smudge and a flat, clear work space. As your child proceeds from item to item, encourage him to ask you if he doesn't understand something. In a real testing situation, questions are accepted, but the extent to which items can be explained is limited. Don't go overboard in making sure your child understands what to do. Your child will have to learn to trust his instincts somewhat.

The test shouldn't take all day. If your youngster seems to be dawdling along, enforce time limits and help him to understand that the real test will have time limits as well. Relax, and try to have fun!

To the Student:

These tests will give you a chance to put the tips you have learned to work.

A few last reminders . . .

- Be sure you understand all the directions before you begin each test. You may ask the teacher questions about the directions if you do not understand them.

- Work as quickly as you can during each test.

- When you change an answer, be sure to erase your first mark completely.

- You can guess at an answer or skip difficult items and go back to them later.

- Use the tips you have learned whenever you can.

- It is OK to be a little nervous. You may even do better.

Now that you have completed the lessons in this book, you are on your way to scoring high!

STUDENT'S NAME		SCHOOL
LAST	FIRST	MI	TEACHER

FEMALE ◯   MALE ◯

Letter grid (A–Z) for each name column.

BIRTHDATE

MONTH	DAY	YEAR
JAN	0 0	0
FEB	1 1	1
MAR	2 2	2
APR	3 3	3
MAY	4	4
JUN	5	5 5
JUL	6	6 6
AUG	7	7 7
SEP	8	8 8
OCT	9	9 9
NOV		
DEC		

GRADE

① ② ③ ④ ⑤ ⑥

Vocabulary

1 Ⓐ Ⓑ Ⓒ Ⓓ 2 Ⓐ Ⓑ Ⓒ Ⓓ 3 Ⓐ Ⓑ Ⓒ Ⓓ 4 Ⓐ Ⓑ Ⓒ Ⓓ

Word Meanings in Context

5 Ⓐ Ⓑ Ⓒ Ⓓ 7 Ⓐ Ⓑ Ⓒ Ⓓ 9 Ⓐ Ⓑ Ⓒ Ⓓ 10 Ⓐ Ⓑ Ⓒ Ⓓ 11 Ⓐ Ⓑ Ⓒ Ⓓ 12 Ⓐ Ⓑ Ⓒ Ⓓ
6 Ⓐ Ⓑ Ⓒ Ⓓ 8 Ⓐ Ⓑ Ⓒ Ⓓ

Spelling

13 Ⓐ Ⓑ Ⓒ Ⓓ 16 Ⓐ Ⓑ Ⓒ Ⓓ 19 Ⓐ Ⓑ Ⓒ Ⓓ 21 Ⓐ Ⓑ Ⓒ Ⓓ 23 Ⓐ Ⓑ Ⓒ Ⓓ 25 Ⓐ Ⓑ Ⓒ Ⓓ
14 Ⓐ Ⓑ Ⓒ Ⓓ 17 Ⓐ Ⓑ Ⓒ Ⓓ 20 Ⓐ Ⓑ Ⓒ Ⓓ 22 Ⓐ Ⓑ Ⓒ Ⓓ 24 Ⓐ Ⓑ Ⓒ Ⓓ 26 Ⓐ Ⓑ Ⓒ Ⓓ
15 Ⓐ Ⓑ Ⓒ Ⓓ 18 Ⓐ Ⓑ Ⓒ Ⓓ

Reading Comprehension

27 Ⓐ Ⓑ Ⓒ Ⓓ 29 Ⓐ Ⓑ Ⓒ Ⓓ 31 Ⓐ Ⓑ Ⓒ Ⓓ 33 Ⓐ Ⓑ Ⓒ Ⓓ 35 Ⓐ Ⓑ Ⓒ Ⓓ 37 Ⓐ Ⓑ Ⓒ Ⓓ
28 Ⓐ Ⓑ Ⓒ Ⓓ 30 Ⓐ Ⓑ Ⓒ Ⓓ 32 Ⓐ Ⓑ Ⓒ Ⓓ 34 Ⓐ Ⓑ Ⓒ Ⓓ 36 Ⓐ Ⓑ Ⓒ Ⓓ 38 Ⓐ Ⓑ Ⓒ Ⓓ

Study Skills

39 Ⓐ Ⓑ Ⓒ Ⓓ 41 Ⓐ Ⓑ Ⓒ Ⓓ 43 Ⓐ Ⓑ Ⓒ Ⓓ 45 Ⓐ Ⓑ Ⓒ Ⓓ 47 Ⓐ Ⓑ Ⓒ Ⓓ 49 Ⓐ Ⓑ Ⓒ Ⓓ
40 Ⓐ Ⓑ Ⓒ Ⓓ 42 Ⓐ Ⓑ Ⓒ Ⓓ 44 Ⓐ Ⓑ Ⓒ Ⓓ 46 Ⓐ Ⓑ Ⓒ Ⓓ 48 Ⓐ Ⓑ Ⓒ Ⓓ 50 Ⓐ Ⓑ Ⓒ Ⓓ

VOCABULARY

Directions: Choose the word that best completes the analogy in the question.

1 Slim is to thin as happy is to _____.

   A sleepy

   B sad

   C joyful

   D gloomy

2 Night is to evening as down is to _____.

   A lower

   B high

   C up

   D over

3 Summer is to hot as winter is to _____.

   A warm

   B shiver

   C boiling

   D cold

4 Day is to night as living is to _____.

   A lively

   B nonliving

   C moving

   D immobile

STOP

WORD MEANINGS IN CONTEXT

Directions: Choose the best definition for the underlined word in the question.

5   The truck had to <u>haul</u> a load of trees from the forest to the paper mill.

   A carry

   B yell

   C leave

   D return

6   The singer became a <u>celebrity</u> when she won a national talent contest.

   A an outcast

   B an astronaut

   C a famous person

   D an unknown person

7   Chocolate chips are an <u>essential</u> ingredient in chocolate chip cookies.

   A unnecessary

   B necessary

   C flimsy

   D sleepy

8   Mrs. Stirling told Michael he needed to <u>apologize</u> to Joshua after he pushed him.

   A smile

   B frown

   C ask forgiveness

   D move away from

9   Joey was <u>fishing</u> for trout in Lake Horace.

   A looking for

   B trying to catch with a pole, bait, and a hook

   C seeking information

   D hunting with a gun

10   Wendy asked Tommy if he could <u>loan</u> her money to buy lunch, and she would pay him back tomorrow.

   A give money that will be returned

   B give money that will not be paid back

   C pay back money

   D steal money

11   Dawna shopped <u>carefully</u> for the perfect gift for David.

   A without care

   B quickly

   C with care

   D without thinking

12   There was a <u>pregame</u> special program of bands and floats.

   A after the game

   B during the game

   C during the advertisements

   D before the game

STOP

SPELLING

Directions: Read each group of words. Choose the word that is spelled correctly.

13   **A**   babys

      B   babyes

      C   babies

      D   babbies

14   **A**   dresses

      B   dresss

      C   dressies

      D   dressys

15   **A**   mouses

      B   mices

      C   meece

      D   mice

16   **A**   moose

      B   meese

      C   mooses

      D   meeses

Directions: Read each sentence. Choose the word that best fits in the blank.

17   Julie made sure she had enough balloons for all the _____.

      A   guest

      B   guests

      C   guestes

      D   guesties

18   Linda wanted to see just one more _____ in the parade before she went home.

      A   float

      B   floats

      C   floates

      D   floatts

19   How many _____ are in Mrs. Gamill's homeroom?

      A   childs

      B   childrens

      C   children

      D   childes

20   Debbie took a picture of six _____ in our backyard last week.

      A   deers

      B   deer

      C   dears

      D   dear

Directions: Choose the correct spelling of the contraction in the questions that follow.

21   should not

      A   should't

      B   should'n

      C   should'nt

      D   shouldn't

GO →

22 will not

   A   willn't

   B   won't

   C   will'nt

   D   wont

23 they are

   A   they're

   B   there

   C   their

   D   theyre'

Directions: Read each sentence. Choose the correct possessive form to fill in the blank.

24 The _____ hat blew off during the night.

   A   snowmen's

   B   snowmans'

   C   snowman's

   D   snowmans

25 Rachel and Natalie went to the _____ house to play for the day.

   A   Millers

   B   Miller's

   C   Millers'

   D   Milleres

26 The British colonists had to use the _____ ships to sail to the New World.

   A   king's

   B   kings

   C   kings'

   D   kinges

STOP

READING COMPREHENSION

Directions: Read each question. Then choose the statement that best answers the question.

27 Which of the following statements is a **fact**?

A Poinsettias are the most beautiful flower.

B The school bought one dozen poinsettias for the holiday play.

C The poinsettias looked sad after the holiday passed.

D White poinsettias are the prettiest ones to have on holidays.

28 Which of the following statements is a **fact**?

A Lucky was an English springer spaniel.

B Springer spaniels are the cutest dogs you can have.

C Brown and white dogs are the most handsome spaniels.

D Everyone should have an English springer spaniel.

29 Which of these statements is an **opinion**?

A Miss Callahan is a fourth-grade teacher.

B Miss Callahan is a nice teacher.

C Miss Callahan has 12 girls in her class.

D Miss Callahan has taught for nine years.

Directions: Read each passage. Then read the questions and choose the best answer.

Felicia sat on the sofa with a cup of hot chocolate. She enjoys this kind of a day. She has watched the white flakes drifting from the sky while she sipped her hot drink. Felicia thought today would be a good day to start reading her new book.

30 In which season does this paragraph take place?

A spring

B summer

C winter

D fall

31 What was Felicia watching drifting from the sky?

A hot chocolate

B cats

C rain

D snowflakes

GO

The students at Central School had only two days before the big performance. The teachers knew the days would be filled with practices and a lot of singing. The children had practiced their songs so much that they were singing the songs while they worked and ate and played.

32 What were the children preparing for?

   A   a math test

   B   a big test

   C   a school play

   D   a car wash

33 When did the children sing their songs?

   A   in their sleep

   B   while they ate

   C   on the bus

   D   walking in the halls

Directions: Read each story and answer each question.

This was the worst day of Ms. Smith's week. It was Friday and the last day of the week, and Ms. Smith was looking forward to a nice quiet weekend at home. When she got to the schoolhouse, she discovered there was no wood in the building for the fire. She had to go outside and walk through the 8 inches of freshly fallen snow to get the wood. It took longer than she thought, and the building was still cold when the children arrived.

As Ms. Smith took attendance, she realized most of her sixth graders were absent because of the snow. This meant her plan to give the history test would have to be postponed until the following week. And then—more trouble at noon! It started to snow again, and she had to send the children home in the middle of the day.

34 Which statement best tells the main idea of this story?

   A   Ms. Smith had to go out in the snow.

   B   Ms. Smith had to send the children home early.

   C   Ms. Smith had a bad day.

   D   Ms. Smith has planned a history test for today.

35 Which of these statements is **not** a supporting detail of the main idea?

   A   Ms. Smith had no wood in the schoolhouse.

   B   The school was not warm when the children arrived.

   C   Ms. Smith loved snow.

   D   Most of the sixth grade was absent.

Lee's favorite book is *Carry On, Mr. Bowditch!* by Jean Lee Latham. It is a historical fiction novel about sailing during the colonial period. The story tells about the life of Nathaniel Bowditch and how he became the captain of a ship. In the book there are exciting stories of adventure out at sea.

36 Which statement is the main idea of the paragraph?

   A   In the book there are exciting stories of adventure out at sea.

   B   Lee's favorite book is *Carry On, Mr. Bowditch!* by Jean Lee Latham.

   C   It is a historical fiction novel about sailing during the colonial period.

   D   The story tells about the life of Nathaniel Bowditch and how he became the captain of a ship.

Directions: Read the story. Use the information in the story to answer each of the questions.

The game was tied 4 to 4. The coach knew it was crucial to the team to win this game. Joey was up at bat. The first two pitches were strikes. Joey wiped the sweat off his brow. The next three pitches were high and outside. Now it was three balls and two strikes.

Joey had to hit this next pitch out of the park. He looked the pitcher right in the eye and took a deep breath as the ball came right at him. He swung with all of his might, and his teammates and the crowd cheered with delight. Joey was a hero!

37 What happened when Joey hit the ball?

   A   He struck out.

   B   He fell down.

   C   He hit a home run.

   D   He hit a foul ball.

38 What kind of ball game is Joey playing?

   A   baseball

   B   football

   C   soccer

   D   tennis

STOP

STUDY SKILLS

Directions: Use the words in each group to answer the questions.

39 Which word would be last in alphabetical order?

   A   catastrophe

   B   caroling

   C   caterpillar

   D   casting

40 Which word would be first in alphabetical order?

   A   quilt

   B   quail

   C   Quebec

   D   quaint

41 Which word would be next in alphabetical order: *magazine, maggot, magnificent,* _____?

   A   mantel

   B   magnify

   C   magic

   D   math

42 Which word would be found on the dictionary page with these guide words: *obstacle / octopus*?

   A   organism

   B   orbit

   C   obtuse

   D   organic

43 Which word would not be on a dictionary page with these guide words: *drain / drape*?

   A   drama

   B   drank

   C   drainage

   D   drop

44 Which dictionary page would the word *substantial* be on?

   A   sulk/summit

   B   submit/subtotal

   C   stall/stand

   D   sand/sink

GO

Directions: The following questions refer to a page from a telephone book reproduced below. Read each question, and choose the correct answer.

C 338 CRAFTS—CREDIT CARDS

© Bell State 2000

CRAFT SUPPLIES

Johnson's Paint Supplies
Art classes, paints, canvas, papers
501 Main Street, Leesport . . . .(800) 555-4457

Kris Kringle Crafts
Craft materials
456 North Main Street . . . .(800) 555-3642

Le Petit Crafter

CRAFT MATERIALS
"Huge collection of beads and feathers"
439 Main Street . . . .(800) 238-0987

Sally's Stamping Store
Rubber stamp supplies
239 Lake Shore Drive . . . .(800) 555-7467

Scrap Book Central
Complete scrap-booking supplies, papers, punches
892 Dunbar Road . . . .(800) 555-2839

Tully's Crafts 2300 Douglas Road . . . .(800) 555-0566

Turner's Kuntry Krafts 39 Red Town Road . . . .(800) 555-9395

Warner's Fabrics 394 Old Mill Road, Milton . . . .(800) 555-0596

GO

45 Look at the telephone book page above. Where would you go to buy supplies to help your mom start rubber stamping?

A   Kris Kringle Crafts

B   Johnson's Paint Supplies

C   Sally's Stamping Store

D   Scrap Book Central

---

46 Which store is on Dunbar Road?

A   Kris Kringle Crafts

B   Johnson's Paint Supplies

C   Sally's Stamping Store

D   Scrap Book Central

---

47 What number would you call to ask about signing up for art classes?

A   (800) 555-4457

B   (800) 555-7467

C   (800) 238-0987

D   (800) 555-2839

Directions: Read each question, and then choose the best answer.

48 Which would you find at the beginning of a reference book?

A   introduction

B   glossary

C   index

D   appendix

---

49 Where would you look to find the meaning of the word <u>medieval</u>?

A   introduction

B   glossary

C   index

D   appendix

---

50 In which part of a book would you look in to find the titles of different chapters?

A   table of contents

B   introduction

C   glossary

D   index

STOP

Answer Key for Sample Practice Test

Vocabulary

1	C
2	A
3	D
4	B

Word Meanings in Context

5	A
6	C
7	B
8	C
9	B
10	A
11	C
12	D

Spelling

13	C
14	A
15	D
16	A
17	B
18	A
19	C
20	B
21	D
22	B
23	A
24	C
25	C
26	A

Reading Comprehension

27	B
28	A
29	B
30	C
31	D
32	C
33	B
34	C
35	C
36	B
37	C
38	A

Study Skills

39	C
40	B
41	B
42	C
43	D
44	B
45	C
46	D
47	A
48	A
49	B
50	A